A GUIDE TO TRACING Y

A GUIDE TO TRACING YOUR DUBLIN ANCESTORS

James G. Ryan

First Published 1988 by:
Flyleaf Press,
4 Spencer Villas,
Glenageary,
Co Dublin,
Ireland.

© James G. Ryan 1988

British Library Cataloguing in Publication Data

Ryan, James G. (James George), 1950-
A guide to tracing your Dublin ancestors.
1. Dublin. Families. Genealogical aspects
I. Title
929'.2'0941835

ISBN O 950846-61-9.

Cover design by: Donal Swift & Associates

Printed in Great Britain by A. Wheaton & Co. Ltd., Exeter

Tracing Ancestors in Ireland

WITH AGENTS IN ENGLAND, SCOTLAND & WALES

Hibernian RESEARCH Company Ltd

IRELAND'S OLDEST & LARGEST RESEARCH COMPANY

Over the past four hundred years millions of Irish have emigrated from their homeland. People of Irish descent can now be found in all the English speaking countries of the world, as well as Continental Europe, Central and South America.

Tracing your ancestors requires competent and conscientious investigation. The members of *Hibernian Research* are professional genealogists with experience in researching all aspects of family history. The company was formed to promote genealogical services and expertise. Anyone interested in tracing their own ancestors now has easy access to a team of genealogists. These professionals have access to the newly computerized records throughout Ireland and also have unrivalled experience in specialist manuscripts and archives, valuable in family research.

All *Hibernian Research* staff have been trained under the direct supervision of the Chief Herald of the Genealogical Office. All *Hibernian Research* staff are members of the Irish Genealogical Research Society, the Association of Professional Genealogists in Ireland, and the Association of Irish Professional Genealogists.

Hibernian Research Co. Ltd. is a panel of professional genealogists with experience in researching all aspects of family history. Hibernian Research is equipped to perform specific research requests for you, or the most thorough and detailed research assignment.

Our research service received worldwide recognition with our completion of the Irish investigations of the ancestry of:

Mary Robinson:	President of Ireland
Ronald Reagan:	former US President
Brian Mulroney:	former Canadian Prime Minister
John E. McEnroe:	Professional Tennis Player
Patrick Duffy:	Star of 'Dallas'
Regis Philbin:	TV Personality

....and thousands of past clients.

~~~~ *Visitors to Ireland* ~~~~

Personal consultations with a genealogist are available by appointment. Please ring our 24 hour answering service 01-496-6522

Hibernian
RESEARCH
Company Ltd

P O Box 3097
Dublin 6 Ireland

Tel: +353-1-496-6522 (24 hrs.)
Fax: +353-1-497-3011
e.g. USA: 011-353-1-496 6522

As Irish surnames are often numerous in several areas it is important that initial research be completed before investigations commence in Ireland.

Facts to seek in your home country:

- Place of origin of ancestor in Ireland (county, parish, townland)
- Approximate dates of birth, marriage, death
- Religious denomination
- Occupation
- Childrens' names (chronologically if possible)

Records to consult in your home country:

- Birth, marriage, death records (civil & parochial)
- Census returns
- Immigration and naturalization papers
- Ship's passenger lists
- Family bibles and traditions

All enquiries must be made to:

Hibernian Research Company Ltd.
PO Box 3097
Dublin 6 Ireland
Tel: +353-1-496-6522 (24hrs.)
Fax: +353-1-497-3011

- *What information is needed to commence family ancestry research?*

  Generally, it is vital to receive as much information as possible from the client, but specifically it is important to have a name, approximate relevant dates (birth, marriage, death), place of ancestor's residence (town, parish, county), and religion.

  See: *Application form.*

- *Are positive results guaranteed and how far back does research extend?*

  Although all Hibernian Research members are professional genealogists, due to the nature of genealogical research positive results cannot be guaranteed. Investigations are highly dependent upon information provided by the client. The extent of research is dictated by available records pertaining to a particular area and family.

- *How long does it take to receive a completed ancestral report?*

  Research will be completed from a minimum of one month to a maximum of four months.

Urgent Investigations

Can be commissioned for an additional fee; please telephone or fax for further information.

For registration and application forms, please complete the following and return with IR£5, (US$5), or equivalent.

Air mail service can have your family search under way immediately.

Personal consultations are available by appointment.

Name: _____

Street: _____

City: _____

State: _____

Country: _____

Postal or Zip Code: _____

Telephone: _____

Please indicate where brochure was obtained:

_____

_____

_____

Member: *Irish Genealogical Research Society*
Association of Professional
  Genealogists in Ireland
Association of Irish Professional
  Genealogists
Dublin Tourism
Mid-Western Tourism
Shannon Tourism
Cork/Kerry Tourism

Contents

Acknowledgements

Thanks are due to the following institutions who provided some of the illustrations used in the text, and who otherwise assisted in compiling the information. To the Trustees of the National Library of Ireland who provided the copies for several of the illustrations used. The Civil Parish maps are also based, with their permission, on those in the library's "Surnames Index". To the Deputy Keeper of Public Records of Ireland for permission to reproduce the sample census return and extracts from their listing of Church of Ireland parish registers; and to the Registrar General's Office for supplying the extract from the Rev. Schulze's records.

Thanks are also due to the Kildare Archaeological & Historical Society for permission to reproduce an extract from their journal, to the Representative Church Body for information on their holdings, and to the Irish Times for permission to reproduce Business notices.

Thanks also to Ms Michelle Power for typing the text, to Mr Gerard O'Connor of Irish Academic Press for his help and advice, and to Mr Robert Welsh, Ancestry Inc, Salt Lake City, USA who provided the map artwork and also assisted in locating records held in the USA.

The photographs on the cover are by courtesy of The National Gallery of Ireland. The Dubliners represented are: *top left:* Mrs Carter Hall (1800-1881); *bottom:* Jonathan Swift (1667-1745) and *right:* Robert Emmett (1778-1803). In the background is the head of Sitric, King of Dublin from 989 to 1036 A.D.

CHAPTER ONE

Introduction

Although Dublin celebrates its 1000th birthday in 1988, the site was inhabited as long ago as 140 AD when Ptolemy noted a settlement here. The city has a long history as a Norse viking settlement, a Norman city, as the centre of English administration of the "reconquered" medieval Ireland and in the 18th century as one of Europe's largest cities.

The city and its suburbs have grown considerably from, for example, a population of some 60,000 in 1682 to its current size of around 1 million inhabitants. It is reasonable to suggest that modern Dubliners include the descendants of the original Dubliners. There are also descendants of the later arrivals to the city i.e. the Irish, Norse, Norman, English, Huguenot and other racial groups. Particularly in the millennium year, there is a natural fascination among Dubliners to know when their family's association with the city began, and what part they may have played in the city's history. This history has been well documented in many publications and will not be repeated here.

This book is designed to assist those who wish to establish their links with those Dubliners who defended, ran and worked the city over the ages, who inspired its writers, artists and leaders, built its great buildings and otherwise contributed to the city's existence and fame.

This guide attempts to present the major sources of family records for the city and county of Dublin. Unfortunately Irish family records for all counties, including Dublin, are sparse. In the time period of greatest interest, i.e. the late 18th and early/middle 19th centuries, most of the rural Irish population (and particularly those who subsequently emigrated) lived as small tenant farmers or labourers. In the urban areas there was also a large labouring, servant and indeed beggar population. These activities gave rise to few written records. Even such events as births and marriages were not generally recorded by the state until 1864. Church records are an important source but many of the Church of Ireland records no longer exist, while those of the Catholic church in most cases do not begin until after 1800. Because of this, every source of information can be valuable to the family researcher. Indeed many of the very best sources of information are those dealing only with one town or parish. A detailed guide to these scattered sources is therefore very valuable to the family record searcher.

The available records for Dublin county and city are listed under the following headings:

◘ Censuses and Census Substitutes
◘ Church Records
    Catholic records
    Church of Ireland records
    Other denominations
◘ Commercial and local directories
◘ Newspapers
◘ Family histories
◘ Wills, Administrations and Marriage Licences.
◘ Gravestone Inscriptions
◘ Archives, Research Services and Local History Sources
◘ Miscellaneous Sources

CHAPTER TWO

How to use this guide

There are no definitive ways of ensuring success in family research. In some cases a researcher can start with a large amount of information on a family's vital data, names and areas of residence and find nothing. In other cases persistent researchers with only the bare essentials of data have, through hard work and creative research, succeeded. Initiative is an important ingredient in finding Irish roots, particularly where family details are sparse. Once the normal sources such as parish registers and land valuation records have been consulted, imaginative use of local historical accounts can produce further information about the family and its circumstances. Alternatively, it can point the way towards other sources of information. In short, the more that is known about life in the area at the relevant period, the more one can try to imagine the ancestors situation and the aspects of their life which might have been recorded.

2.1 Principles for family research

This guide is designed to facilitate family research by providing a comprehensive listing of all the major record sources in Dublin city and county. The objective of the family researcher is to add to the stock of information about his/her ancestors from the records available. This essentially means adding more "elements of identity" to their ancestors. Elements of identity are names, dates, places and relationships which distinguish one person from another and thus help to ensure that the researcher is following the right lines. For example, if a researcher knows only that his ancestor was a Michael Farrell born in Dublin city in the early 1830's it would be very difficult to establish a definite family line because there were many people of that name born at that time and place. If the exact birth date, or place, is known, then the possibilities are greatly improved.

The principles on which this should be done are simple.

(a) Work from what is already known to what is unknown. The researcher should concentrate on adding to the known elements of identity of their ancestors. The best approach is to work on the ancestor about whom most is known. By adding new elements of identity to this person, more information will inevitably be found about the other earlier relatives, siblings etc. What the researcher should not do is to find a family of the same name in the ancestors area and try to establish a link. Many Irish family names are associated with particular areas and therefore many of the same name can be expected to be found. An exception to this rule is where the name is very rare and a linkage therefore reasonable. Build from what is already known and, if the apparently ''right'' family is found, test the accuracy, e.g. by looking for evidence of the named person after the records suggest he/she had died or left the country.

(b) Work from the more recent events in the ancestors life to the less recent. As records generally improve with time, it may for example, be easier to find a person's birth date by looking at death records and gravestone inscriptions. In the case of emigrant ancestors, both of these principles suggest that all possible information on the person in the immigrant country should be collected before attempting to trace ancestry in Ireland.

2.2 What the records can tell

The following is a guide to the information types, or elements of identity, which various sources can provide:

Where did they live?

A precise ''address'' for an ancestor is one of the most valuable elements of identity, particularly in searching for ancestors with names which are locally very common. Records which provide both names and definite addresses are therefore very valuable ways of linking people with places. The two major records used for these purpose are the Griffith Valuation Survey (see p. 21) in the mid 1800's and the Tithe Applotment Survey (see p. 21) in the early 1800's. Unfortunately, neither of these apply to the city of Dublin, although they do cover the remainder of the county.

Both these records are indexed in the ''Surname Index'' compiled by the National Library of Ireland. In this index you can find out how many house/land holders with a particular family name were recorded in the Griffith Survey, and also whether (but not how many) landholders of that name are in the Tithe Applotment Survey. By examining the original records indicated in the index the full names of those listed and the townland in which they lived can be established.

A further useful source for Dublin city and other towns is commercial directories of which there is a very good selection (see Chapter 5).

For the latter part of the 19th century, a good source is the civil register of births, deaths and marriages. Full registration started in 1864, but Church of Ireland marriages are registered from 1845 onwards. If, for instance, it is known when the parent of an ancestor died, the death certificate may give the family home address. Marriage certificates are particularly useful as they give the addresses of both partners.

There are a range of other censuses and census substitutes listed (see Chapter 3), some of which have names arranged alphabetically and give addresses.

Who were their relations?
If an address has been found, the most obvious way of identifying other family members is to check local church records of birth and marriage. To do this it will be necessary to identify the church which served the area and consult its records, if they exist. This can be done using the guides in Chapter 4.

After 1864, official certificates of death, birth and marriage are also available (Church of Ireland marriage certificates are available from 1845). Marriage certificates give the names of the bride's and groom's fathers. Death records are less useful since they only list the name of the person present at death, whose relationship is often not stated. Birth certificates give the names of both parents, including the maiden name of the mother.

Other useful sources include Gravestone inscriptions (see p. 77) Wills (see p. 71), marriage license bonds (see p. 74), and newspaper birth, marriage and death notices (see p. 59). A few of the more detailed censuses (see p. 19) also list entire households and give relationships among those within. Finally, there are pedigrees and family histories (see p. 68). These exist mainly for more prominent families.

2.3 Irish Placenames and Family Names

Place-names
The majority of Irish place-names, and particularly townland names, are derived from the Gaelic, or Irish, language. A good description of the origins of Irish placenames is given in *Irish Names of Places* (1893), and *Irish Local Names Explained* (1884, reprinted 1979) both by P.W.

Joyce. Because these names are ancient there are often variations in the way in which they are spelt, particularly in earlier documents. Some imagination is therefore necessary to relate these names to their currently accepted forms.

Finding a Place-Name
To find a place name there are several good sources. In compiling censuses during the last century, indexes of townlands were compiled and are available. These are:

Alphabetical Index to the Towns and Townlands of Ireland. Dublin: Alexander Thom and Co., 1877: This lists townlands alphabetically and gives, for each, the parish, barony, county and poor law union to which it belongs. The parishes, baronies and poor law unions are also listed separately.

General Alphabetical Index to the Townlands and Towns, Parishes and Baronies of Ireland. 1851. (Reprinted by Baltimore Genealogical Publishing Co. Inc., 1984). Based on the 1851 census, this gives much the same information as the above index.

Having found where an ancestor lived, some further background information on the area may be got from the following publications:

Topographical Dictionary of Ireland by Samuel Lewis (1837). This lists all the parishes, baronies, towns, villages and counties in Ireland with local administrative details, an account of agriculture and industry, major local houses ("seats") and their owners, and other local information.

Parliamentary Gazetteer of Ireland, published by Fullerton and Co. (1846) gives much the same information as the above.

Street names can be located in most of the later commercial directories, particularly Thom's (see Chapter 5). Note that "Terrace" is very often a row of houses within a street with a different name e.g. Clanbrassil Terrace and Tyrconnell Terrace are both on South Circular Road. They will not usually be listed separately in census records etc. Note also that streetnames have been changed on many occasions in Dublin for commemorative or political reasons. If the street of interest is not listed on modern street indexes, consult an older Thom's Directory which will indicate the location of the street by reference to connecting streets (see also Chapter 11).

Local history journals are also a good source of information on the history and other aspects of particular areas of Dublin. The Irish Place-Names Commission in the Ordnance Survey Office (see below)

ALPHABETICAL INDEX TO THE TOWNLANDS AND TOWNS OF IRELAND. 281

No. of Sheet of the Ordnance Survey Maps.	Townlands and Towns.	Area in Statute Acres.	County.	Barony.	Parish.	Poor Law Union in 1857.	Townland Census of 1851, Part I.	
		A. R. P.					Vol.	Page
3	Commons Upper	243 0 3	Dublin	Balrothery West	Garristown	Dunshaughlin	I.	22
11, 15	Commons Upper	243 0·30	Kildare	South Salt	Lyons	Celbridge	I.	77
88	Commons West	30 1 19	Cork, E.R.	Imokilly	Cloyne	Middleton	II.	85
114	Commons West	581 1 28	Cork, W.R.	Bear	Kilcatherine	Castletown	II.	124
11	Commons West	48 0 6	Dublin	Nethercross	Swords	Balrothery	I.	32
125	Commons West	380 2 12	Galway	Leitrim	Ballynakill	Loughrea	IV.	51
20	Commons West	61 0 4	Kerry	Clanmaurice	Ardfert	Tralee	III.	167
5	Commons West	41 1 14	Kildare	Ikeathy&Oughterany	Kilcock	Celbridge	I.	57
9	CommonThe,orSralahan	207 1 3	Cavan	Tullyhaw	Tomregan	Bawnboy	III.	96
32	Comraghs	207 0 12	Monaghan	Farney	Inishkeen	Dundalk	III.	271
13, 14	Conagher	1,385 1 16a	Fermanagh	Magheraboy	Inishmacsaint	Ballyshannon	III.	212
4	Conagher	813 3 21	Galway	Dunmore	Dunmore	Tuam	IV.	33
15	Conaghil	296 0 0	Leitrim	Drumahaire	Drumlease	Manorhamilton	IV.	94
16	Conaghoo	78 0 18	Cavan	Tullygarvey	Annagh	Cootehill	III.	87
6	Conaghra	461 3 4	Mayo	Tirawley	Doonfeeny	Killala	IV.	167
7	Conaghra	204 0 4	Mayo	Tirawley	Lackan	Killala	IV.	170
36, 37	Conaghrud	306 2 6	Donegal	Kilmacrenan	Tullyfern	Milford	III.	133
12	Conaghy	182 2 26	Monaghan	Dartree	Killeevan	Clones	III.	267
22	Conavalla	778 1 18b	Wicklow	Ballinacor North	Knockrath	Rathdrum	I.	347
15	Concaroe	61 0 37	Fermanagh	Magheraboy	Devenish	Enniskillen	III.	212
6	Concealment	87 1 29	Cork, E.R.	Orrery and Kilmore	Kilbolane	Kanturk	II.	108
22	Concealment	350 2 22	Kildare	Offaly West	Lackagh	Athy	I.	73
9	Concess	232 3 14	Tyrone	Strabane Lower	Ardstraw	Strabane	III.	318
40	Conckera	165 2 39c	Monaghan	Clankilly	Galloon	Clones	III.	198
20, 25	Concra	319 2 32	Monaghan	Cremorne	Clontibret	Castleblayney	III.	260
64	Condonstown	71 0 12	Cork, E.R.	Barrymore	Ballycurrany	Middleton	II.	51
55	Condonstown	431 0 27	Cork, E.R.	Barrymore	Clonmult	Middleton	II.	53
35	Condonstown	322 1 25	Kilkenny	Knocktopher	Aghaviller	Thomastown	I.	110
53	Condonstown North	547 3 3	Cork, E.R.	Barrymore	Kilshanahan	Fermoy	II.	56
53	Condonstown South	512 1 9	Cork, E.R.	Barrymore	Kilshanahan	Fermoy	II.	56
19, 24	Condry	139 3 7d	Cavan	Tullyhunco	Killashandra	Cavan	III.	97
22	Conerick	222 1 17e	Fermanagh	Tirkennedy	Trory	Enniskillen	III.	223
6, 7	Cones	1,293 1 34	Queen's Co.	Tinnahinch	Rearymore	Mountmellick	I.	249
52,53,63,64	Coneybeg	449 0 4	Cork, E.R.	Barrymore	Templeusque	Cork	II.	59
71	Coneyburrow	130 1 14f	Donegal	Raphoe	Clonleigh	Strabane	III.	134
35	Coneyburrow	9 1 25	Kildare	Narragh & Reban West	St. Johns	Athy	I.	68
35	Coneyburrow	85 1 36g	Kildare	Narragh & Reban West	St. Michaels	Athy	I.	68
11	Coneyburrow	79 2 0h	Kildare	South Salt	Donaghcumper	Celbridge	I.	76
18	Coneyburrow	72 2 11	Louth	Ardee	Cappoge	Ardee	I.	171
12	CONEYBURROW T.	—	King's Co.	Coolestown	Monasteroris	Edenderry	I.	133
20	Coneygar	235 0 38	Kilkenny	Gowran	Clara	Kilkenny	I.	94
2	Coney Island	2 1 4	Armagh	Oneilland West	Tartaraghan	Lurgan	III.	16
50, 60	Coney Island	245 0 13	Clare	Clonderalaw	Killadysert	Killadysert	II.	16
148	Coney Island	6 1 14	Cork, W.R.	West Carbery (W.D.)	Skull	Skull	II.	146
46	Coney Island	13 1 34	Donegal	Raphoe	Allsaints	Londonderry	III.	134
45	Coney Island	48 0 24	Down	Lecale Lower	Ardglass	Downpatrick	III.	178
39	Coney Island	15 0 0	Fermanagh	Knockninny	Kinawley	Lisnaskea	III.	203
42	Coney Island	3 2 22	Londonderry	Loughinsholin	Ballyscullion	Magherafelt	III.	240
7, 8, 13, 14	Coney Island or Inishmulclohy	388 0 12	Sligo	Carbury	Killaspugbrone	Sligo	IV.	222
11, 12	Coneykeare	124 1 24	Carlow	Idrone West	Wells	Carlow	I.	10
87	Coney or Rat Island	0 0 39	Cork, E.R.	Barrymore	Templerobin	Cork	II.	59
6, 11	Confey	947 0 16	Kildare	North Salt	Confey	Celbridge	I.	74
120	Cong North	12 3 31	Mayo	Kilmaine	Cong	Ballinrobe	IV.	153
28	Congo	42 0 37	Fermanagh	Magherastephana	Aghalurcher	Lisnaskea	III.	215
46	Congo	214 1 29j	Tyrone	Dungannon Middle	Drumglass	Dungannon	III.	302
120	Cong South	9 3 0k	Mayo	Kilmaine	Cong	Ballinrobe	IV.	153
120	CONG T.	—	Mayo	Kilmaine	Cong	Ballinrobe	III.	154
37, 38,44,45	Coniamstown	424 2 15	Down	Lecale Upper	Bright	Downpatrick	III.	180
105	Conicar	117 1 29	Galway	Dunkellin	Kilconickny	Loughrea	I.	29
116,117,126	Conicar	125 2 32	Galway	Leitrim	Ballynakill	Portumna	IV.	51
42	Conicker	185 1 33	King's Co.	Clonlisk	Ettagh	Roscrea	I.	130
19, 20	Conigar	267 1 34	Limerick	Connello Lower	Lismakeery	Rathkeale	II.	228
4, 5, 12, 13	Conigar	513 0 14	Limerick	Pubblebrien	Mungret	Limerick	II.	254
8	Coniker	161 2 3	King's Co.	Ballycowan	Durrow	Tullamore	I.	127
15	Conlans Hill	78 3 24	Wicklow	Lower Talbotstown	Hollywood	Baltinglass	I.	360
17	Conlanstown	262 1 18	Kildare	Offaly East	Cloncurry	Naas	I.	65
10	Conlanstown	549 0 2	Westmeath	Moygoish	Kilmacnevin	Mullingar	I.	280
38, 42	Conleen	103 1 9	Cavan	Clanmahon	Kilbride	Oldcastle	III.	77
2,6	Conlig	637 1 4	Down	Ards Lower	Bangor	Newtownards	III.	157
2, 6	CONLIG T.	—	Down	Ards Lower	Bangor	Newtownards	III.	157
69	Conloon	280 2 19	Mayo	Carra	Turlough	Castlebar	IV.	130
17	Conly Island	64 3 34	Down	Dufferin	Killinchy	Downpatrick	III.	166

(a) Including 17A. 3R. 31P. water.
(b) Including 2A. 3R. 2P. water.
(c) Including 12A. 3R. 2P. water.
(d) Including 7A. 1R. 5P. water.
(e) Including 40A. 3R. 0P. water.
(f) Including 4A. 0R. 4P. water.
(g) Including 5A. 1R. 24P. water.
(h) Including 3A. 2R. 16P. water.
(i) Including 2A. 1R. 16P. water.
(j) Including 3A. 3R. 29P. water.
(k) Including 2A. 2R. 22P. water, and 1A. 3R. 31P. detached portion.

2 O

Sample page from the townland index of the "Alphabetical index to the townlands and towns of Ireland", Thom's, Dublin 1861 (reprinted, Baltimore 1984).

can usually assist in finding the accepted variant for difficult place-names or street names where the above sources fail.

Maps are available from different periods depending on need. Xerox copies of the Griffith Valuation Survey maps (County Dublin only) are available from the Valuation Office, 6 Ely Place, Dublin 2. These show the boundaries of the holdings of each of those listed in the survey itself. A full set of 19th century maps of a wide range of scales are also available for consultation at the National Library of Ireland.

A wide range of scale maps of Dublin are available from the Ordnance Survey Office, Phoenix Park, Dublin 8. The following historical maps are also available; "Dublin c. 840 to c. 1540: The years of medieval growth", by P.J. Walshe (1977), which shows the medieval town; and "The Medieval Town in the modern City" by H.B. Clarke (1978) which shows the medieval features imposed on a modern city map. A reproduction of Rocque's 1756 Map of Dublin is also available from the Ordnance Survey Office.

A map of Dublin showing "where the Huguenots first prospered and the particular places that some of the prominent members of the Dublin Huguenot community lived and worked", is available from Learáid Maps, 159 Glenageary Park. Glenageary, Co. Dublin.

Family Names

Irish family names are mainly derived from Gaelic and Norman names. English and Scottish names are also common, particularly in Dublin. Most Scottish names are also derived from Gaelic. Huguenot, Palatine and Jewish names also occur. To complicate the situation, many English surnames or family names were adopted by Irish families during the 17th and 18th centuries when Irish names were discouraged. MacGowan, for instance, became Smith, and McDarra became Oakes by translation, or mistranslation, of the original names

The spelling of Irish surnames also varies (e.g. Keogh, Kehoe; O'Mara, O'Meara; O'Loughlin, O'Lochlann, O'Loghlen). Thus it is often necessary to establish the accepted local spelling of a name before searching. A modern Irish telephone directory is one useful way to find the currently accepted forms of names. In general terms the spelling form used currently in Ireland is more likely to be the form of spelling used in 18th and 19th century records. This is not always the case however.

A good source for determining variants of family names is Edward McLysaghts *Surnames of Ireland* and his other books *Irish Families, More Irish Families* etc. Another source is Robert E. Matheson's *Special*

RINGSEND, a small town, in that part of the parish of St. Mary, Donnybrook, which is in the county of the city of Dublin, in the province of Leinster, 1½ mile (E.) from the General Post-office : the population is returned with the parish. This place, according to O'Halloran, was originally called *Rin-Aun*, signifying, in the Irish language, "the point of the tide," from its situation at the confluence of the Dodder with the Liffey; its present name is either a singular corruption of the former, or may perhaps have arisen from the large blocks of stone into which rings of iron were inserted for mooring vessels, previously to the construction of the present mole. The town is built upon the eastern bank of the Dodder, and has a mean and dilapidated appearance, having fallen into decay since the discontinuance of its extensive salt-works : its southern portion, which is a few hundred yards detached, is called Irishtown, and is in a less ruinous condition; it is much frequented for sea-bathing, from its proximity to Dublin. There are also hot and cold sea-water baths ; the Cranfield baths, which are here much frequented, are said to have been the first hot sea water baths erected in Ireland. Iron-works were established here by the grandfather of the late proprietor, Mr. C. K. Clarke· by whom they have been recently disposed of : the articles manufactured are steam-engines and all kinds of machinery, iron boats and utensils of various kinds. There are also glass-works, a chymical laboratory, and a distillery. The Grand Canal Company have docks to the west of this place, opening a communication between the canal and the river Liffey. Ship-building is carried on, and many of the inhabitants are employed in the fishery. Along the whole of the shore are strong embankments to keep out the sea, which at high water is above the level of the town; and similar precautions are taken to prevent inundation from the river Dodder, which frequently overflows its banks. In 1649, Sir William Ussher, though attended by many of his friends, was drowned in crossing this dangerous stream, over which a bridge of stone was afterwards erected; but the river suddenly changed its course and rendered it useless, till the stream was again forced into its former channel. In 1796, the corporation for improving the port of Dublin diverted the stream into a new channel through the low grounds between Irishtown and Dublin; and in 1802 the bridge was destroyed by a flood, and a handsome bridge of granite, of one arch, was erected, over which the road by the docks to Dublin is carried. A church was built in Irishtown, in 1703, under an act of the 2nd of Queen Anne, on account of the distance from the parish church and the difficulty of access from the frequent inundation of the roads.

A description of Ringsend, now an inner Dublin suburb, from Lewis'
"Topographical Dictionary of Ireland" 1839.

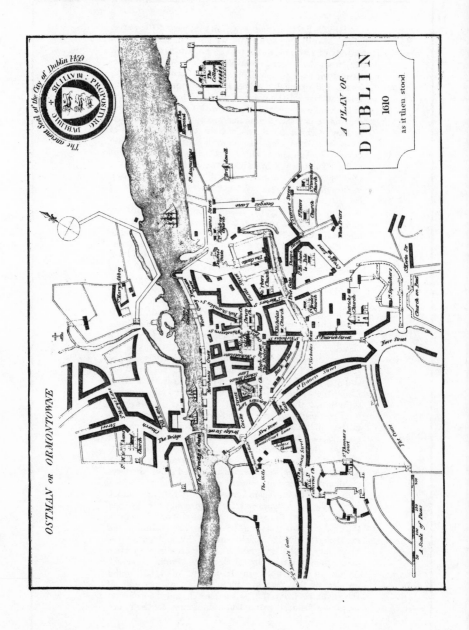

Report on Surnames in Ireland together with Varieties and Synonyms of Surnames and Christian Names (1901); reprinted by Baltimore Genealogical Co.

A common variation in Irish names is whether they have an 'O' or 'Mac' prefix. During the 18th and 19th centuries, when the Irish language died away in most of the country, there was a gradual dropping of the 'O' and to a lesser extent 'Mc' from names. During the latter half of the century, when awareness of Gaelic heritage grew, these prefixes were restored. Thus when searching relevant names it is wise to check both forms (e.g. Sullivan and O'Sullivan, Neill and O'Neill).

2.4 Administrative Divisions

An ancestors address is a basic element of identity as well as being an essential step in obtaining further information. To understand the components of the types of "addresses" commonly cited, it is necessary to know about the administrative areas used.

Many different administrative boundaries were used in Ireland for civil and ecclesiastical purposes. In most cases these divisions observe boundaries set up for other purposes e.g. county boundaries, but others e.g. dioceses, do not. A short description of the different divisions is given below. A more detailed description is given by Dr. W. Nolan in *Irish Genealogy — A Record Finder* (Heraldic Artists, Dublin, 1981).

Civil Divisions:
These are described below starting from the smallest unit of land.

Townland: This is the smallest unit of land area used in Ireland. The area varies in size from less than 10 acres to several thousand acres. Despite their name they do not necessarily contain towns, indeed some have no occupants at all. There are around 64,000 townlands in Ireland and they are the most specific "address" usually available for rural dwellers. They are generally organized into civil parishes.

Civil parishes: These are important units for record purposes. They generally contain around 25-30 townlands as well as towns and villages. There are 83 Civil parishes in Dublin county and a further 19 in Dublin city. The guide to church records (see Chapter 4) lists these parishes, and they are also shown in the maps on pages 29 and 30. Parishes are generally listed within each county although they may also be divided by Barony. In some cases civil parishes straddle county and barony boundaries.

Barony: A Barony is a portion of a county, or a group of civil parishes. Historically it was introduced by the Anglo-Normans and is usually based on a tribal territory or "tuatha". Barony boundaries do not always conform to those of the civil parishes within them. There are 10 Baronies in Dublin (see p. 28).

Boroughs and Wards: These are separate administrative areas of varying size. A Borough is a town with a corporation, or alternatively a town which sent a representative (i.e. M.P.) to the Westminster Parliament. A Ward is an administrative unit within a city or large town.

Ecclesiastical Divisions

The Church Parish is the basic area over which a parish priest or minister presided. Church of Ireland parishes generally conformed to the civil parish boundaries. Catholic parish boundaries, which are generally larger, do not. The guide to Catholic church records shows the Catholic parish(es) to which each civil parish belonged before 1880.

The *Diocese* is the area presided over by a Bishop and consists of many parishes. The boundaries do not conform to any civil divisions but Dublin city and county is entirely within the Diocese of Dublin for both the Church of Ireland and Catholic church.

CHAPTER THREE

Census and Census Substitutes

This section includes censuses and various types of census substitutes. The latter are records which are not official censuses but fulfill the same function by listing local inhabitants for various military, religious or taxation purposes. The different types of census substitutes are described below. Official censuses are described first and then each other type in the approximate chronological order of its occurrence.

(a) Official Government Censuses of the entire population of Ireland were first conducted in 1821 and subsequently at 10 year intervals. Although the statistical information from each census is available, few individual household returns for Dublin city or county are available for any years other than 1901 and 1911. Almost all of the returns for the other years were destroyed either by Government order (1861 to 1891) or in the fire which destroyed the Public Record Office in 1922. The returns for 1901 are a very valuable source of information since they provide names, ages and relationship to the head of household of each resident person.

Also recorded is the county of birth of each member of the household. This is particularly useful in attempting to trace the origins of those who migrated to Dublin from other parts of the country.

(b) Civil Survey: Following the defeated rebellion of the Irish catholics of 1641, there was a massive confiscation of the tribal lands and their redistribution to English adventurers (i.e. those who had provided the funds to raise the army which put down the rebellion), soldiers (as payment for services) and other groups. The Civil Survey was conducted in 1654/56 and listed the owners of land in 1640, and the new owners. The parts which survive have been published by the Irish Manuscripts Commission.

(c) Hearth Money Rolls: In the 1660's a tax was levied on Ireland payable on the basis of the number of hearths (i.e. fireplaces) in each house. It gives the householders names in each parish for which the records survive.

CENSUS OF IRELAND, 1901.

(The Examples of the mode of filling up this Table are given on the other side.)

No. on Form B.

FORM A.

RETURN of the MEMBERS of this FAMILY and their VISITORS, BOARDERS, SERVANTS, &c., who slept or abode in this House on the night of SUNDAY, the 31st of MARCH, 1901.

Sample Dublin Household Return from the 1901 Census of Ireland
(courtesy Deputy Keeper of Public Records of Ireland).

(d) Census of Ireland (1659): This gives the names of "tituladoes" i.e. those with title to land, and total number of persons overall. It also lists the numbers of families in each barony with Irish names.

(e) Catholic Qualification Rolls: After 1692 a series of so-called "Penal laws" were enacted which severely restricted the rights of catholics in land and property ownership, and in almost all other areas of activity. These restrictions were gradually lifted towards the end of the 18th century for those catholics who took an oath of allegiance and thereby "qualified". In 1778, for example, those taking the oath could take long-term land leases. In 1782 it allowed the buying and selling of land by catholics. The "rolls" consist of those taking the oath. In Dublin the number taking the oath is relatively small (98).

(f) Religious Censuses: In several dioceses, and in some parishes, censuses of parishioners were taken at various times (e.g. in 1749 for Elphin Diocese, 1766 for Meath Diocese etc). These were in some cases for ecclesiastical administration purposes and in others for security reasons as catholic or "popish" was at many times in Irish history equated to "rebel". The censuses vary widely in quality and accuracy.

(g) Freeholders lists: A freeholder was one who held land for life or for several lives, as distinct from short-term leaseholders, or annual rentpayers. The significance of freeholder status is that they were the major group which was entitled to vote. Several of the Dublin lists give addresses and other useful details.

(h) Tithe Applotment Survey: Tithes were a form of tax payable by all religious denominations for maintenance of the Church of Ireland which was the "established" church, i.e. the state recognized church, until 1867. Between 1823 and 1837 a valuation was conducted to determine the tithe payable by each eligible local landholder. Tithes were only payable on certain types of land and the Tithe Applotment Survey is therefore far from comprehensive. It does not include any urban inhabitants for instance. However, it is nonetheless a valuable source for Dublin county. The surnames in the survey have been indexed (see Griffith Valuation below).

(i) Griffith's Valuation Survey: Between 1848 and 1864, all of Ireland

was surveyed for the purpose of establishing the level of rates (i.e. local tax) to be paid by each landholder or leaseholder. It lists each land, or house, holder in the country giving the townland and description of the property (e.g. land; house; house and land; or house, outoffices (i.e. outbuildings) and land). It also lists the landlord and the annual valuation. Because of the shortage of other records this is a very important substitute census although it obviously does not cover all inhabitants of an area. It is particularly important in emigrant family research as it was carried out during a period when much emigration occurred and thus it can form a useful link between the information available about the local origins of an emigrant ancestor and the Irish records. The names occurring in this and the Tithe Applotment Survey have been indexed in the National Library's "Surnames Index". This, however does not cover the city of Dublin but it does include the remainder of the county.

(j) Local Censuses and Map Indices: For some towns and districts there are detailed censuses, the reasons for which are sometimes obscure. Detailed maps, particularly estate maps, of some areas also give the names of holders of land shown.

(k) Lists of Freemen: The status of Freeman of specified cities and towns was given to citizens whom the city wished to honour. They were therefore generally prominent citizens or visitors. However, as this status also conferred voting rights, it was abused in some pieces so as to admit voters for certain candidates or parties.

(l) Estate Rentals: The vast majority of small farmers and town-dwellers rented their properties from large land-owners, many of whom lived abroad. The records of these estates can include details of their tenants. The records are scattered and highly variable in value. Only a small number of the available rentals are listed in this book. Estate rentals will often list only the Estate's principal tenants, i.e. those from whom the estate directly collected rent. These tenants would, in turn, have rented to sub-tenants.

To trace estate rentals it is first necessary to find the name of the ancestor's landlord, e.g. through Griffiths Valuation Survey (see i). A search for the estate records etc. or family papers can then be made e.g. through Richard J. Hayes "Manuscript Sources for the History of Irish Civilization" (NLI). Other Estate Papers and records in private hands

Barony

Meehan	G6	T	Uppercross
Meehan	G		Dublin
Meehan	G3		Rathdown
Meek	G		Rathdown
Meekins	G	T	Rathdown
Mehegan	G		Uppercross
Meldon		T	Castleknock
Meldon	G		Rathdown
Meleady	G		Castleknock
Meledy	G		Rathdown
Melia		T	Uppercross
Mellefont		T	Rathdown
Mellin	G		Coolock
Mellington	G		Rathdown
Melyn	G		Rathdown
Memory	G		Rathdown
Mercer	G		Coolock
Meredith	G		Castleknock
Meredith	G		Coolock
Meredith	G2		Rathdown
Mergan	G	T	Uppercross
Merigan	G		Uppercross
Merins	G		Castleknock
Merna	G		Dublin
Merner	G		Rathdown
Merrick	G		Newcastle
Merrick	G		Rathdown
Merrigan	G		Uppercross
Merrigan	G2	T	Rathdown

Extract from the "Index to surnames of Householders in Griffith's Primary Valuation and Tithe Applotment Books for Co. Dublin" National Library of Ireland 1967. The columns show the family name, number of Holdings listed in Griffith's Survey (e.g. G6), whether or not the name occurs in the Tithe Applotmnent book (i.e T or blank) and the Barony in which the name occurs. The occurence of these names in the civil parishes within each barony is similarly shown elsewhere in the same volume. (Courtesy of the Trustees of the National Library of Ireland).

are listed in Analecta Hibernica, volumes 15, 20 and 25. From 1849 to 1885 the estates of insolvent owners were sold at public auction. Auction notices generally listed properties and tenants names. These records of "Encumbered Estates", indexed by landlord's name, are available in the NLI and PRO.

(m) Voters lists: Lists of voters, particularly in the large towns and cities are available for various periods. A large number of lists relating to those entitled to vote was produced as evidence for the "Commission on Fictitious Votes" in 1837/38. These include lists of Freemen, Marksmen (i.e. those entitled to vote by making a mark rather than a signature) and other lists for Dublin city.

Years	Description and Source of Record
1468-'85 & 1575-1774	Roll of Freemen of the City of Dublin. NLI Mss 76-79; & GO Ms 490-493; SLC Film 100228.
1621	List of householders in St. John's parish who were rated for parish cess. Appendix II in the **Registers of St. John's 1619-1699**, Parish Register Society, 1906 Vol. I. p. 273; SLC Film 824047.
1646	List of householders for St. John's parish. Parish Register Society Vol. I (1906) p. 276; SLC Film 824047.
1652	Inhabitants of the Baronies of Newcastle and Uppercross, districts of Ballyfermot, Balliowen, Ballidowde, Belgard, Bellemount, Blundestown, Butterfield, Carranstown, Crumlin, Dalkey, Deane Rath, Esker, Feddenstown, Finstown, Gallanstown, Great Katherins, Irishtown, Killnemanagh, Killiney, Kilmainham, Kilmactalway, Kilshock, Loughstown, Lucan, Milltown, Nanger, Nealstown, Newcastle, Newgrange, Newland, Oldbawn, Palmerstown, Rathgar, Rathfarnham, Rowlagh (Ranelagh), Rockstown, Shankill, Symon, Tallaght, Templeogue, Terenure. (gives names, ages, occupations and relationships). PRO 1A 41 100.
1654-6	Civil Survey, Vol. VII. Irish Manuscripts Commission.

PARISH OF DRUMCONDRAH.

Clanturke	Lawrence Barrett	one hearth	ii
	John ffanninge	one hearth	ii
	Lawrence Liddey	one hearth	ii
	James Murphey	one hearth	ii
	Donnogh Doyle	one hearth	ii
	Phelim Law	one hearth	ii
	Murtagh Dowlinge	two hearths	iiii
	William Christee	one hearth	ii
	Thomas Scolley	one hearth	ii
	Nicholas Patrick	two hearths	iiii
	Hugh Welsh	one hearth	ii
	Andrew Patrick	one hearth	ii
	Patr. Cawan	one hearth	ii
Drishoge	John Griffin	three hearths	vi
	Gordg (?George) Patrick	one hearth	ii
	Richard Cleere	one hearth	ii
	Tirlaugh Quinn	one hearth	ii
Grangedanliffe	Robert Munnes	eight hearths	xvi
Dunnecarny	William Bazell, Esq.	eight hearths	xvi
	John Jackson	two hearths	iiii
	William Waringe	one hearth	ii
Ballebought	Andrew Cane	three hearths	vi
	William Tilch	one hearth	ii
	Thomas Bourke	one hearth	ii
	Henry Lake	one hearth	ii
	David Normend	one hearth	ii
	Gilbert Cavanagh	one hearth	ii
Drumcondrah	George Carter	one hearth	ii
	William Powell	one hearth	ii
	John Eyres	one hearth	ii
	John Smith	one hearth	ii
	William Erly	one hearth	ii
	Andrew Lyons	one hearth	ii
	John Allen	one hearth	ii
	Nicholas Boyland	one hearth	ii
	Richard Doyle	one hearth	ii
	Richard Eaths	one hearth	ii
	Lewis Powell	one hearth	ii
	Hugh	one hearth	ii
	Toby	one hearth	ii
	David	one hearth	ii

Extracts from the 1663 Hearth Money Roll for County Dublin from the "Journal of the Kildare Archaeological Society", Vol 11.

Years	Description and Source of Record
1659	"Census" of Ireland. Ed. by S. Pender, Stationery Office, Dublin 1939.
1663	Hearth Money Roll. **Kildare Arch. Soc.** J. Vol. 10(5), p. 245-254, and 11(1) pp. 386-466. (also covers parts of Kildare).
1687	List of householders in St. John's parish. Parish Register Soc. Vol. I (1906) p.277; SLC Film 824047.
1766	Religious census of Parishes of Crumlin, Donnybrook, Castleknock and Taney. RCB Library: SLC Film 258517 (except Donnybrook).
1767	List of freeholders in Co. Dublin. PRO M.4912.
1774-1824	Alphabetical list of the Freemen of the City of Dublin. **Ir. Anc.** 15(1) and (2), 1983, p. 2-133.
1775	Catholic Qualification roll extracts (98 names, addresses and occupations). 59th Rept. **DKPRI**, pp. 50-84.
1777-1830	Brethren admitted to the Guild of Smiths, Dublin, by marriage right, 1777-1830. **Reports from Committees (Parl. Papers)**, 1837, Vol. II (ii) pp. (480) 182.
1778-1782	The Catholic Merchants, manufacturers and traders of Dublin 1778-1782. Reportorium Novum 2(2) 1960, p. 298-323. (Compiled from Catholic qualification rolls; gives name, trade and address).
1792-1837	Names of all persons admitted to Dublin trade guilds eg Apothecaries, Bakers, Barbers, Surgeons, Carpenters, Smiths, Merchants, Tailors, etc., 1792-1837. **Parl. Papers**, 1837, Vol.11 p. 161-191: Appendix 3 (gives names, some father's and father's-in-law names).
1793-1810	Census of Protestants in Castleknock. GO Ms. 495; SLC Film 100225.
1798	List of Persons who suffered losses in '98 rebellion. NLI. JLB 94107 (approx. 100 names, addresses and occupations).

Year	Description and Source of Record
1820	Freemen of Dublin who voted at a Parliamentary election. Arranged alphabetically by candidate chosen. Also list of "Neutral" freemen. (name, residence and occupation). NLI P734.
1821	Government Census extracts for Dublin City and Tallaght for selected surnames. SLC Film 100158; PRO.
1823-37	Tithe Applotment Survey.
1824	See 1774.
1830	See 1777.
1830	Dublin City and County freeholders: (names and addresses). NLI Ms 11.847.
1831	Householders in St. Bride's parish (Possibly based on 1831 Government census) NLI P.1994.
1832	Number and names of Freemen registered as voters, City of Dublin, **Parl. Papers**, 1837, Vol. II(1) pp. 159-175. (2678 names only).
1832-36	An alphabetical list of the registered voters in Parliamentary elections for the City of Dublin. **Parl. Papers**, 1837, Vol. II (ii), p. (480) 1-145. (names, occupations, residence etc. given alphabetically by year of registration).
1832-36	Names and residences of persons in Dublin receiving liquor licenses. **Parl. Papers**, 1837, 11(i) Appendix 11, p. 250.
1835-37	Dublin County freeholders and leaseholders 1835, 1837 and 1852. NLI MS.9363.
1837	See 1792
1848-51	Griffith's Valuation (see p. 21) (The parishes of Dublin city are not included in the Index to Surnames).
1852	see 1835-37.
1901	Government Census, PRO
1911	Government Census, PRO

Baronies of Dublin County

1. BALROTHERY, EAST
2. BALROTHERY, WEST
3. NETHERCROSS
4. CASTLEKNOCK
5. COOLOCK
6. NEWCASTLE
7. UPPERCROSS
8. DUBLIN
9. RATHDOWN

← DUBLIN CITY

Index to Civil Parish Map — Dublin County

1. Balscaddan
2. Balrothery
3. Skerries or Holmpatrick
4. Lusk
5. Baldongan
6. Naul
7. Garristown
8. Grallagh
9. Hollywood
10. Ballymadun
11. Palmerston
12. Clonmethan
13. Westpalstown
14. Ballyboghil
15. Killossery
16. Swords
17. Donabate
18. Portraine
19. Kilsallaghan
20. Killeek
21. Ward
22. Mulhuddart
23. Cloghran
24. Finglas
25. Clonsilla
26. Castleknock
27. Chapelizod
28. Malahide
29. St Margaret's
30. Santry
31. Cloghran
32. Kilsaley
33. Portmarnock
34. Balgriffin
35. Coolock
36. Baldoyle
37. Glasnevin
38. Clonturk
39. Artaine
40. Raheny
41. Kilbarrack
42. Howth
43. Grangegorman
44. St George's
45. Killester
46. Clontarf
47. Leixlip
48. Lucan
49. Aderrig
50. Esker
51. Kilmactalway
52. Kilmahuddrick
53. Kilbride
54. Newcastle
55. Rathcoole
56. Saggart
57. Palmerstown
58. Clondalkin
59. Ballyfermot
60. St James'
61. Drimnagh
62. Crumlin
63. St Catherine's
64. St Peter's
65. Tallaght
66. Cruagh
67. St Mark's
68. Donnybrook
69. Rathfarnham
70. Taney
71. Booterstown
72. Whitechurch
73. Kilmacud
74. Stillorgan
75. Monkstown
76. Tully
77. Kill
78. Dalkey
79. Kilgobbin
80. Killiney
81. Kiltiernan
82. Rathmichael
83. Old-Connaught

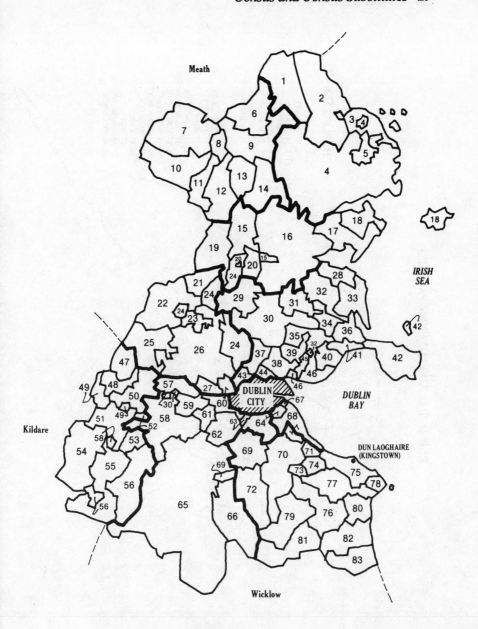

Meath

Kildare

Wicklow

IRISH
SEA

DUBLIN
BAY

DUN LAOGHAIRE
(KINGSTOWN)

DUBLIN
CITY

= CIVIL PARISHES ADJOINING ACROSS
BARONY BOUNDARIES.

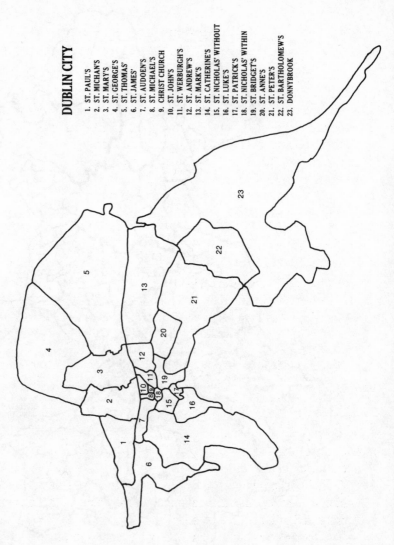

DUBLIN CITY AND ADJOINING PARISHES

DUBLIN CITY

1. ST. PAUL'S
2. ST. MICHAN'S
3. ST. MARY'S
4. ST. GEORGE'S
5. ST. THOMAS'
6. ST. JAMES'
7. ST. AUDOEN'S
8. ST. MICHAEL'S
9. CHRIST CHURCH
10. ST. JOHN'S
11. ST. WERBURGH'S
12. ST. ANDREW'S
13. ST. MARK'S
14. ST. CATHERINE'S
15. ST. NICHOLAS' WITHOUT
16. ST. LUKE'S
17. ST. PATRICK'S
18. ST. NICHOLAS' WITHIN
19. ST. BRIDGET'S
20. ST. ANNE'S
21. ST. PETER'S
22. ST. BARTHOLOMEW'S
23. DONNYBROOK

CHAPTER 4

Church Records

Because of the lack of census information, church records are the most important source of information on family relationships. This information is in the form of baptismal, marriage and, occasionally, burial records. Note that Civil registration of these events took place from 1864 (see p. 11). The value, quality and accessibility of the records of each religious denomination are discussed here:

4.1 Catholic Church Records

Church records are undoubtedly the most important record source for Catholics. However, because the Catholic church was severely restricted in the 18th century under the penal laws, there were few well-appointed churches and therefore few records in most of the country. Dublin, however has some of the earliest records in the country. Seven churches have records dating before 1750 and 22 are pre-1800.

For doctrinal reasons, catholic children were baptised as soon as feasible after birth and usually in a church if there was one. On the other hand, except for the very poor, marriages of catholics were generally conducted in the bride's home. Marriage records are therefore less likely to be accurate than baptismal records. Catholic churches in Dublin Diocese usually did not keep death or burial records although they do occur in some other dioceses.

Catholic record books have been microfilmed and are available in the National Library, the Genealogical Office and at the Genealogical Library in Salt Lake City in the USA.

The records themselves are highly variable in terms of legibility of handwriting, level of detail and state of preservation. At worst, the handwriting can be virtually illegible, written in Latin using the writer's own abbreviations, and give only the most basic information, e.g. a baptismal record might give the date followed by "Patrick of James & Honora Murphy". In addition, the ink may be faded, the register book may be torn at the edges, overwritten or have pages missing. At best the records are written in beautiful copperplate handwriting in neat columns, giving full details (e.g. date and "Patrick, of James Murphy, Carpenter, and Honora Bennett of Tullowcanna") in well preserved books. All possible combinations of these variables will be found. Names of witnesses are almost always given and these may sometimes give clues as to other family associations.

The Catholic records for Dublin county and city are listed in the following pages. The records are listed according to the civil parish in which the church is situated. The maps referred to are those on pages 29 (County Dublin parishes) and 30 (Dublin City parishes). This is the most useful means of organizing the information because the Catholic parish serving any particular area may have changed as new churches were built and the older parishes reduced in size. Unless the area of residence is very clearly within a specific Catholic parish, it is wise to check all the neighbouring parishes for records.

The earliest record dates are also indicated (month & year) and the dates for which records are missing. The original record books are usually kept at the parish office or church and are usually not directly accessible to the public. Parish clergy understandably cannot give priority to record searching and it is usually preferable, where possible, to consult the records on microfilm at the National Library of Ireland or elsewhere. Some Dublin church records are still not available on microfilm and a direct approach to the parish is therefore the only option.

Catholic Church Records — Dublin County

Civil Parish	Map Ref	Name of Church or Parish	Earliest Records	Dates for which no records exist	Parish Address
Aderrig	49	see Lucan			
Artaine	39	see Clontarf			
Baldongan	5	see Skerries			
Baldoyle	36	Baldoyle	b.12.1784 m.1.1785	12.1800-8'06 12.1800-8'06; 11'15-5'18; 11'24-1'26	Rev. Canon G. Finnegan, P.E., 76 Grange Road, Baldoyle, Dublin
Balgriffin	34	see Baldoyle			
Ballyboghil	14	see Balrothery			
Ballyfermot	59	see Lucan			
Ballymadun	10	see Garristown			
Balrothery	2	Balrothery & Balbriggan	b.10.1816 m.2.1817		Rev. James O'Sullivan, PP, Parochial House, Balbriggan, Co. Dublin
Balscaddan	1	see Balrothery			
Booterstown	71	Booterstown * (also see below)	b.1755 m.1756		Rev. Jerome Curtin, PP, Parochial House, Booterstown, Co. Dublin
Booterstown	71	Blackrock * (also see below)	b.1850 m.1922		Rev. D. Henry, CC. 35 Newtown Ave. Blackrock, Co. Dublin
Booterstown	71	Dundrum *	b.1861 m.1861		Rev. J. Fagan, PP, The Presbytery, Main St. Dundrum, Dublin 14.
Castleknock	26	Blanchardstown	b.12.1774 m.1.1775		Rev. S. McGeehan, PP, Parochial House, Blanchardstown, Dublin 15
Chapelizod	27	Chapelizod: * (see Clondalkin for earlier records)	b.1846 m.1846		Parochial House, Chapelizod, Dublin. 20

* Records not on microfilm — available only from parish.

Civil Parish	Map Ref	Name of Church or Parish	Earliest Records	Dates for which no records exist	Parish Address
Cloghran (near Castleknock)	23	see Castleknock			
Cloghran (near Santry)	31	see Clontarf			
Clondalkin	58	Clondalkin	b.5.1778 m.6.1778	4.1800-8'09; 2. 1800-8'12	Rev. M. Ryan, PP. St. Cecilia's, New Rd., Clondalkin, Dublin 22
Clonmethan	12	Rowlestown, see Killossery			
Clonsilla	25	see Castleknock			
Clontarf	46	Clontarf *	b.1774 m.1774		Rev. J. Gunning, 68 Clontarf Rd. Clontarf, Dublin 3.
Clonturk (or Drumcondra)	38	Fairview, (see Clontarf for earlier records)	b.6.1879 m.6.1879		Rev. W. Rogan, PP, Presbytery, Fairview, Dublin
Coolock	35	Coolock * (see Clontarf for earlier records)	b.1879 m.1879		Rev. P. O'Farrell, PP., St. Brendan's Presbytery, Coolock, Dublin 5.
Cruagh	66	see Rathfarnham			
Crumlin	62	see Rathfarnham			
Dalkey	78	Dalkey (see Monkstown for earlier records)	b.1861 m.1894		Rev. J. Meagher, St. Joseph's, Dalkey Ave, Dalkey, Co. Dublin
Donabate	17	Donabate	b.11.1760 m.1.1761	12.1807-7.'24 6.1805-2.'69	Rev. D. O'Kane, PP., Parochial Hse. Donabate, Co. Dublin
Donnybrook	68	part Donnybrook, see Dublin City; part Booterstown			
Drimnagh	61	see Clondalkin			
Dublin City		see separate listing and map			
Esker	50	see Lucan, Palmerstown & Clondalkin			

Civil Parish	Map Ref	Name of Church or Parish	Earliet Records	Dates for which no records exist	Parish Address
Finglas	24	Finglas & St. Margaret's	b.2.1784 m.11.1757	7.1760-12.1784	Rev. W. Deasy, P.P. Parochial Hse. Finglas, Dublin 11
Garristown	7	Garristown	b.1.1857 m.7.1857		Rev. J. K. Dempsey, PP., Parochial Hse. Garristown, Co. Dublin
Glasnevin	37	St. Michans (see Dublin city)			
Grallagh	8	see Garristown			
Grangegorman	43	see St. Paul's (Dublin city)			
Hollywood	9	see Garristown, or Balrothery			
Holmpatrick	3	Skerries	b.10.1751 m.6.1751		Rev. L. Shanahan, PP. Cuan Phadraig, South Strand, Skerries, Co. Dublin
Howth	42	Howth * (see Baldoyle for early records)	b.1890 m.1890		Rev. Brian Kelly PP., Mount Saint Mary's, Howth, Co. Dublin
Kilbarrack	41	see Baldoyle			
Kilbride	53	see Lucan, Palmerstown and Clondalkin			
Kilgobbin	79	Sandyford, see Taney			
Kill	77	Cabinteely,* also part Booterstown	b.1859 m.1859		Rev. George O'Sullivan, PP., Parochial House, Cabinteely, Co. Dublin
Killeek	20	see Finglas			
Killester	45	see Finglas			
Killiney	80	Kingstown, see Monkstown			

* *Records not on microfilm — available only from parish.*

Civil Parish	Map Ref	Name of Church or Parish	Earliest Records	Dates for which no records exist	Parish Address
Killossery	15	Rowlestown	b.1.1857 m.1.1857		Rev. P. Crowley, PP. Parochial Hse. Rolestown, Kilsallaghan, Co. Dublin
Kilmactal-way	51	see Lucan, Palmerstown and Clondalkin			
Kilmacud	73	see Booterstown; also part Kingstown			
Kilma-huddrick	52	see Lucan, Palmerstown and Clondalkin			
Kilsall-aghan	19	part Finglas; also part Rowlerstown, see Killossery			
Kiltiernan	81	Sandyford, see Taney			
Kilsaley	32	see Baldoyle			
Leixlip	47	Maynooth, Co Kildare	b.8.1814 m.1.1806		St Mary's Presbytery, Maynooth, Co Kildare
Lucan	48	Lucan (part of Clondalkin)	b.9.1818 m.9.1818	7'34-8'35; 8'42-2'49; ends 1'62 9'42-2'49	Rev. Donal Coghlan, PE., Main Rd.., Lucan, Co. Dublin
Lusk	4	Lusk (see also below)	b.9.1757 m.11.1757	8'01-3'02; 12'35-8'56 1.'01-3.'02 12.'35-3.'56	Rev. William Warner, PE., Parochial House, Lusk, Co. Dublin
Lusk		Rush	b.9.1785 m.9.1785	12.1796-12.1799 4'10-8'13	Rev. T. Randles, PP,St Francis, Whitestown, Rush, Co. Dublin
Malahide	28	see Swords			
Monkstown	75	Kingstown; * part Booterstown & part Cabinteely, see Kill; see also below	b.1769 m.1769		Rev. C. Mangan, PP, 4 Eblana Ave., Dun Laoghaire, Co. Dublin.

Records not on microfilm — available only from parish.

Civil Parish	Map Ref	Name of Church or Parish	Earliest Records	Dates for which no records exist	Parish Address
Monkstown		Monkstown *	b.1881 m.1867		Parochial House, Carrickbrennan Rd Monkstown, Co Dublin
Mulhuddart	22	see Castleknock			
Naul	6	see Balrothery			
Newcastle	54	Newcastle-Lyons * See also Saggart	b.1773 m.1773		Rev Tadhg McCarthy, PP, The Glebe, Newcastle, Co Dublin
Old-Connaught	83	Kingstown, see Monkstown			
Palmerston	11	Rowlestown; see Killossery			
Palmerstown	57	Palmerstown (part of Clondalkin)	b.8.1798 m.9.1837	12.1799-9'37 ends '62 ends 9'57	Rev. V. Kelly, PP, Parochial Hse. Palmerstown Dublin 20.
Portmarnock	33	see Baldoyle			
Portraine	18	see Donabate			
Raheny	40	see Clontarf			
Rathcoole	55	see Saggart			
Rathfarnham	69	Rathfarnham * (see also below)	b.1771 m,1771		Rev. P. Tuohy, PP. St. Mary's, Rathfarnham, Dublin 14
Rathfarnham		Terenure *	b.1870 m.1894		Rev. John H. Greehy, PP., 83 Terenure Road East, Dublin 6.
Rathmichael	82	Sandyford, see Taney			
Saggart	56	Saggart	b.10.1832 m.5.1832		Rev. L. O'Sullivan, PP., Parochial Hse. Saggart, Co. Dublin.
St Catherine's	63	See Dublin City			
St George's	44	See Dublin City			

* Records not on microfilm — available only from parish.

Civil Parish	Map Ref	Name of Church or Parish	Earliest Records	Dates for which no records exist	Parish Address
St James'	60	See Dublin City			
St. Marks	67	Donnybrook, see Dublin City			
St. Margarets	29	see Finglas			
St. Peter's (also below)	64	Rathmines * (see St. Nicholas Without (Dublin City) for earlier records)	b.1823 m.1823		Rev. Aidan Burke, PP. 54 Lower Rathmines Road, Dublin 6.
St. Peter's		Rathgar * (see Rathmines or earlier records)	b.1874 m.1874		Rev. John Molony, PP., 50 Rathgar Road, Dublin 6.
Santry	30	see Clontarf			
Stillorgan	74	see Booterstown			
Swords	16	Swords	b.12.1763 m.10.1763	7.1777-6'02 6.1777-6'02	Rev M O'Reilly, PP., Parochial Hse. Seatown Road, Swords, Co. Dublin
Tallaght	65	see Rathfarnham			
Taney	70	Sandyford *; also part Kingstown, see Monkstown, also part Booterstown	b.1823 m.1823		Rev. Patrick Corridan, PP., Parochial House, Sandyford, Co. Dublin
Tully	76	Kingstown, see Monkstown			
Ward	21	see Finglas			
Westpals-town	13	see Naul			
Whitechurch	72	see Garristown			

4.1 Roman Catholic Church Records Dublin City Civil Map

Civil Parish	Map Ref	Name of Church or Parish	Earliest Records	Dates for which no records exist	Parish Address
Donnybrook	23	Sandymount * (see Haddington Road, below for earlier records)	b.1865 m.1865		Rev. P. Rice, PP., 76 Tritonville Rd., Dublin 4.
-	23	Donnybrook * (see Haddington Road, below for earler records)	b.1871 m.1877		Rev. Richard Sherry, PP., Presbytery, Stillorgan Road, Dublin 4.
-	23	Haddington Rd.*	b.1798 m.1798		Rev. B. O'Sullivan, PP., The Presbytery, Haddington Road, Dublin 4.
Dublin: Christ Church	9	See St. Nicholas Without			
Dublin: St. Andrews	12	St. Andrew's part St Michael & St. John's	b.1.1742 m.2.1742		Rev. Desmond Dockery, Adm., 47 Westland Row, Dublin 2.
Dublin: St. Anne's	20	see Dublin: St. Andrew's			
Dublin: St. Audoen's	7	St. Audoen's	b.12.1778 m.2.1787	12.1799-6.1800 9'56-6'78 8.1785-1.1800	Rev. John Fitzpatrick St. Audoen's, High Street, Dublin 8.
Dublin: St. Bartholomew's	22	See Donnybrook			
Dublin: St. Bridget's	19	part Michael & John's; part St. Nicholas-Without			
Dublin: St. Catherine's	14	St. Catherine's	b.5.1740 m.5.1740	2.1794-12.1797; 7'66-6'71 12.1792-2.1794 7.1794-12.1799	Rev. Philip Kelly, PP., Parochial House, Meath Street, Dublin 8.
Dublin: St Georges	4	See St. Mary's			

Civil Parish	Map Ref	Name of Church or Parish	Earliest Records	Dates for which no records exist	Parish Address
Dublin: St James'	6	St. James'	b.1742 m.1754	9.1798-1'03 1755-10'04	Rev. Gerald Healy, PP., Parochial House, James's Street, Dublin 8.
Dublin: St. John's	10	see St. Michael's			
Dublin: St. Luke's	16	see St. Nicholas-Without			
Dublin: St. Mark's	13	see St. Andrew's			
Dublin St Mary's (also below)	3	St. Mary's Pro-Cathedral;* also part St. Michan's	b.1734 m.1734		Presbytery, 83 Marlboro St., Dublin 1.
Dublin: St. Mary's (also below)	3	Seville Place: (see St. Mary's for earlier records)	b.7.1853 m.6.1856		Rev. John Stokes, PP. Parochial House, Seville Place, Dublin 1.
Dublin: St. Mary's	3	N. William St.,(see St. Mary's for earlier records)	b.12.1852 m.1.1853		Rev. Michael Smythe, CC., Presbytery, North William Street, Dublin 1.
Dublin: St. Michael's	8	Michael & John's	b.1.1768 m.1.1784 index from 1743 to 1842		Rev. Oscar O'Leary, PP., Adam & Eve's, Merchant's Quay, Dublin 8.
Dublin: St. Michan's	2	St. Michan's; also part St Paul's see also below	b.1726 m.1726		Rev. Donal O'Mahony, PP., Parochial House, Halston Street, Dublin 7.
Dublin: St. Michan's	2	Berkeley Rd * (see St. Michan's for earlier records)	b.1890 m.1890		Rev. Patrick Mulcahy, PP., The Presbytery, Berkeley Road, Dublin 7.

Civil Parish	Map Ref	Name of Church or Parish	Earliest Records	Dates for which no records exist	Parish Address
Dublin: St. Nicholas-Within	18	part Michael & John's: see St. Michael's; part St. Nicholas-Without			
Dublin: St. Nicholas-Without (also below)	15	St. Nicholas-Without	b.1.1742 m.9.1767	8.1752-1.1767 12'01-11.'24	Rev. Desmond O'Beirne, PP., Parochial House, Francis Street, Dublin 8.
Dublin: St. Nicholas-Without	15	Harrington St	b.1865		Rev. D. O'Neill, PP., Parochial House, Harrington St., Dublin 8.
Dublin: St. Patrick's	17	See St.Nicholas Without			
Dublin: St. Paul's	1	St. Pauls'; part St. Michan's; see also below	b.1731 m.1731		Rev. Donal O'Mahony, PP., Parochial House, Halston St., Dublin 7.
Dublin: St. Paul's	1	Cabra: * (see St. Paul's for earlier records)	b.1909 m.1856		Rev. John Moroney, PP., 116 New Cabra Road, Dublin 7.
Dublin: St. Paul's	1	Holy Family * (Aughrim St.) see St Pauls for earlier records	b.1888 m.1888		Rev. Brendan Lawless, PP., Parochial House, 34 Aughrim Street, Dublin 7
Dublin: St Peter's	21	part St. Nicholas-Without; part St. Andrew, part Haddington Rd, See Donnybrook			
Dublin: St Thomas'	5	see St. Mary's			
Dublin: St. Werburgh's	11	Michael & John's see St. Michael's			

* *Records not on microfilm — available only from parish.*

S. JOHN, DUBLIN.   123

September, 1667.

Ellizabeth daughter to John Weauer, esqr., bap.	7
Margarett daughter to Richard Peeters, bap.	9
Mary daughter to Richard Patience, bap.	17
Ellizabeth daughter to William Aderton,	20
Mary daughter to Henry Maruin, bap.	23
William sonn to Christopher Hoskins, bap.	27

October, 1667.

Richard sonn to Nicholas Thomas, bap.	10
Mary daughter to Daniell Trauers, shooemaker, bap.	20
Dennis sonn to Dauid Boy, baptized	29

November, 1667.

John sonn to John Johnson, baptized	7
David sonn to Dauid Phillipps, bap.	16
Sarah daughter to George Knight, bap.	20
Cordela daughter to Edmond Rely, bap.	26

December, 1667.

Katherin daughter to William Burlacy, bap.	5
Thomas sonn to Dauid Lingard, bap.	8
Benjamin sonn to Peter Tribbett, bap.	19
Sarah daughter to Henry Hunter, bap.	29

January, 1667.

Samuell sonn to Thomas Ashly, baptized	7
Gregory sonn to George Byrne, baptized	12
Martha daughter to John Nevill, bap.	19
John sonn to David Jones, bap.	27

ffebruary, 1667.

William sonn to William Mowland, bap.	5
William and James sonns to Richard Hayse,	10
Joseph sonn to John Anderson, baptized	17
Margarett daughter to Roger Courtlogh, bap.	27

March, 1667.

Zachary sonn to John Henderson, baptized	1st
Ellizabeth daughter to Robert Sheron, baptized	6
Mary daughter to Joseph Katherins, bap.	15
Owen and Jane children to Evan Dauis, bap.	18
John sonn to Marks Beacham, baptized	28

Extract from the "Register of St John the Evangelist, Dublin 1619-1699", Parish Register Society, Dublin 1906.

4.2 Church of Ireland Records

These records generally start earlier than Catholic records, the earliest being 1619. Although there was a legal obligation on the Church of Ireland to keep records from 1634, in practise most began after 1750. In 1876 a law was enacted that all registers be sent for sake-keeping to the Public Record Office in Dublin. This was later amended to allow ministers with suitable storage to keep their own registers. Other ministers sent copies or kept copies of their books., Almost all of the registers sent to the PRO, approximately half of those then in existence, were destroyed in the 1922 fire.

The current position is that records are available from several possible sources. The first is the local parish, in the circumstance that the original, or a copy, survives. Many earlier registers had been published by the Parish Register society and are available in libraries. Copies of record books, or parts of record books, may also be available at the Representative Church Body (RCB) Library, at the Public Record Office (PRO), the Genealogical Office (GO), Trinity College Dublin (TCD) Library or the National Library of Ireland (NLI). Note that Church of Ireland marriages were registered in the civil registry from 1845 onwards, and births and deaths from 1864 (see p. 11).

Unlike the Catholic Parishes, Church of Ireland parishes tend to conform to civil parish boundaries. These parishes are listed below with details of whether, and where, copies survive. The Dublin city list is mainly based on that compiled by E.J. McAuliffe and published in the Irish Genealogist.

Church of Ireland Records — Dublin City

Civil Parish	Existing Records	Where held
Christchurch Cathedral	b. 1740-1838/1860-1886	Local Parish
	m.1717-1826	
	d.1710-1866	
Christchurch (Leeson Park)	b. 1867-1879	Local Parish
St Andrew	m. 1672-1819	Published by Parish Reg. Soc.
		(Vol 12), also PRO (M) 5135.
	b/m/d. 1695-1803	(some entries) TCD Ms 2062
St Ann (Dawson St)	m. 1719-1800	Published by Parish Reg. Soc.
	b.1719-1800	GO Ms. 577
	m.1799-1822	GO Ms. 577
	d. 1722-1822	GO Ms. 577
St Audoen	b/m/d. 1673-1885	Local Parish
	m. 1672-1800	Published by Parish
	d. 1672-1692	Reg. Soc. (Vol 12)
St Bride	m. 1639-1800	Published by Parish Reg. Soc.
		(Vol 11)
	b. 1633-1801	TCD Ms. 1478
	m. 1653-1800	TCD Ms. 1479
	d. 1634-1801	TCD Ms. 1480
St Catherine	b/m/d. 1679-1898	Local Parish, also
	b/m/d. 1636-1715	Published by Parish
	m.1715-1800	Reg. Soc.
	d. 1829-1898	Gilbert Library, Pearse St.
St George	b/m/d. 1794-1875	Local Parish
St James	b/m/d. 1736-1872	Local Parish
	b.1742-1796	RCB Library Ms. T35
	m. 1742-1830	RCB Library Ms T36
	b. 1730-1836	NLI P. 6014
	m. 1742-1834	NLI P. 6014
	d. 1742-1836	NLI P. 6014
St John	b/m/d. 1619-1699	Held at St Werburgh's
	m. 1700-1798	& published by Parish Reg. Soc.
		(Vol 1 & 11)
	b/m. 1702-1878 (few)	GO Ms 577
	d. 1621-1850	GO Ms. 577
St John (Sandymount)	b. 1850-1876	Local Parish
St Jude	b. 1857-1876	Local Parish
St Kevin's	See St Peter's	
St Luke	b/m/d. 1713-1875	Local Parish
	m. 1716-1800	Published by Parish Reg. Soc.
St Mark	b/m/d. 1730-1875	Local Parish
	m. 1730-1750	NLI Ms. 18319
St Mary	b/m/d. 1697-1875	Local Parish
	m. 1697-1800	Published by Parish
		Reg. Soc. (Vol 11)
	b/m/d. 1831-1870	PRO 1A.49.59

Civil Parish	Existing Records	Where Held
St Mary (Donnybrook)	b/m/d. 1712-1870	Local Parish
St Matthias	b. 1867-1955	RCB Library
	m. 1873-1955	RCB Library
St Michael	b/m/d. 1656-1800	Published by Parish Reg. Soc. (Vol. 11)
	b/m/d. 1750-1780	Published in "Irish Builder" (1891)
St Michan	b/m/d. 1636-1701	Published by Parish Reg. Soc. (Vols 3, 7 & 11)
	m. 1700-1800	,,
	b/d. 1700-1724	GO Ms. 577
	b. 1701-1787	Extracts at RCB Library
	m. 1706-1809	Extracts at RCB Library
	d. 1727-1745	Extracts at RCB Library
St Nicholas-Within	b/m/d. 1671-1866	Held at St Audoen's
	b/m/d. 1671-1866	(Copy) TCD Ms. 178.R.27
	m. 1671-1800	Published by Parish
	d. 1671-1863	Reg. Soc. (Vol 11)
St Nicholas-Without	b.1694-1861	Held at St Lukes
	m. 1694-1875	Held at St Lukes
	b/m/d. 1694-1739	Published by Parish Reg. Soc. (Vol 10)
St Patrick's Cathedral	b/m/d. 1699-1800	Held in Local Parish, also published by Parish Reg. Soc. (Vol 2)
St Paul	b/m/d. 1698-1982	RCB Library
	d. 1702-1892	Local Parish, also RCB Library
	d.1702-1718	Published by Parish Reg. Soc.
	d. 1719-1821	PRO 1A.37.51
	d. 1718-1730	GO Ms. 577
SS Peter & Kevin	b/m/d. 1669-1883	RCB Library.
	b/m/d. 1669-1761	Pub. by Parish Reg. Soc. (Vol. 9).)
	b. 1669-1813 (few)	TCD Ms. 2602
	m. 1677-1813 (few)	TCD Ms. 2602
	d. 1669-1811 (few)	TCD Ms. 2602
St Stephen's	b. 1837-1866	Held at RCB Library
	m. 1862-1864	Held at RCB Library
St Thomas	b/m/d. 1750-1875	Held in local Parish (damaged from 1800)
	b/m. 1750-1931	RCB Library
	d. 1762-1882	RCB Library
St Werburgh	b/m/d. 1704-1880	Held in Local Parish
	m. 1704-1800	Published by Parish Reg. Soc.

Civil Parish	Existing Records	Where Held
Royal Hospital (Kilmainham)	b. 1826-1879 d. 1849-1879 (also deaths — 1789-1833)	Held by Office of Public Works, Royal Hospital, Kilmainham

Church of Ireland Records — Dublin County

Civil Parish	Period of Records	Where Held
All Saints, Newtown Pk	b. 1870-79	Local parish
Balbriggan	b. 1838-75 m. 1838-71 d. 1821-71	Local parish
Baldoyle		See Howth
Balrothery	b/m/d. 1782	None survive
Blackrock	See Carysfort	
Blanchardstown	See Castleknock	
Booterstown	b. 1824-1875 m. 1824-1845	Local parish
Carysfort (Blackrock)	b. 1855-1878	Local parish
Castleknock	b. 1709-1875 m. 1710-1740/1768-1845 d. 1709-1742/1772-1875	Local parish '' ''
Chapelizod	b/m/d. 1812-1875	Local parish
Cloghran	b. 1782-1870 m. 1738-1839 d. 1732-1870 b. 1870-1891 m. 1858-1875 d. 1872-1938	Local parish (copy) PRO PRO RCB Library RCB Library RCB Library
Clondalkin	b/m/d. 1728-1845	Local parish
Clonmethan	b. 1834- m. 1841- d. 1838-	None survive '' ''
Clonsilla	b/d. 1830-1875 m. 1831-1844	Local parish ''
Clontarf	b. 1807-1875 m. 1811-1852 d. 1811-1875	Local parish, also PRO on microfilm
Coolock	b/d. 1843-1875 m. 1843-1845	Local parish (copy)
Crumlin	b/m. 1740-1832 b/d. 1740-1874 m. 1823-1863	Pub. by Parish Reg. Soc. Vol. 12 Local Parish (copy) PRO

Civil Parish	Period of Records	Where Held
Dalkey	b. 1841-1877	None survive
Donabate	b/d. 1811-1875	Local parish
	m. 1811-1845	
Donnybrook	m. 1845-1956	RCB Library
Drimnagh	See Clondalkin	None survive
Drumcondra	b. 1810-1877	None survive
	m. 1814-1873	
	d. 1792-1874	
Dundrum	See Taney	
Baggotrath	b. 1865-79	St Stephen's parish
Harold's Cross	No records before 1871	Local parish
Holy Trinity, Rathmines	b. 1850-1875	Local parish
St Matthew (Ringsend)	b/d. 1812-1872	Local parish
St Philip (Milltown)	b. 1844-1876	Local parish
Sandford	b. 1826-1880	Local parish
Finglas	b/m/d. 1664-1729	Pub by Parish Reg. Soc. (Vol 11) No others survive
Garristown	b. 1842-	None survive
Glasnevin	b/m/d. 1778-1875	Local parish
Grangegorman	b/m/d. 1816-1875	Local parish
Hollywood	b/m/d. 1813-	None survive
Holmpatrick	b/m/d. 1779-1875	Local parish
Howth	b. 1804-77	Local parish
	m. 1823-1871	,,
	d. 1807-1875	,,
Irishtown	b. 1813-1973	RCB Library
	m. 1824-1956	RCB Library
	d. 1807-1866	RCB Library
Kenure	b/d. 1867-75	Local parish
Kilbarrack	See Howth	
Kilbride	See Clondalkin	
Kill	b. 1863-1890	None survive
Killesk	See Swords	
Killiney	b/d. 1829-1878	Local parish
Kilmactalway	See Clondalkin	
Kilmacud	See Stillorgan	
Kilsallaghan	b/m/d. 1818-1875	Local Parish
Kiltiernan (earlier entries at Bray, Co. Wicklow	b/m/d. 1817-1880	Local Parish
Kingstown (now Dun Laoghaire)	b. 1852-1879	Local parish
Kinsealy	See Swords	
Lusk	b/m/d. 1809-1875	Local Parish
Malahide	b/m/d. 1822-1875	Local Parish

Civil Parish	Period of Records	Where Held
Mariner's Church, Kingstown	b. 1843-1875	Local parish
Milltown (St Philip's)	b. 1844-1876	
Monkstown	b. 1680-1785, 1804-75	Local Parish
	m. 1669-1785, 1804-45	Local Parish
	d. 1676-1785, 1804-75	Local Parish
	b/m/d. 1699-1786	Pub. by Parish Reg. Soc. (Vol 6)
Monkstown (St John)	b. 1860-1875	Local Parish
Mulhuddart	See Castleknock	
Naul	See Hollywood	
Newcastle-Lyons	b. 1768-1847	RCB Library
	m. 1773-1946	RCB Library
	d. 1776-1847	RCB Library
Portmarnock	b/m/d. 1820-	None survive
Raheny	b/m/d. 1815-1875	Local Parish
Rathcoole & Tassagard	b/m/d. 1724-	None survive
Rathfarnham	b/m/d. 1780-	,,
Rathmichael	b. 1865-1891	Local parish (copy)
	d. 1864-1875	,,
Rathmines (Holy Trinity)	b. 1850-1875	Local parish
Ringsend (St Matthew)	b/d. 1812-1872	Local Parish
Rotunda Chapel	b. 1860-1870	Local Parish
Saggart	See Rathcoole	
St Jude	b. 1857-1876	Local parish
St Margaret	See Finglas	
St Paul, Glenageary	b. 1869-1890	None survive
Santry	b/m/d. 1753-1875	RCB Library
Stillorgan & Kilmacud	b/m/d. 1820-	None survive
Swords	b/m/d. 1705-1875	Local parish
Tallaght	b/m/d. 1711-	None survive
Taney	b. 1741-1875	Local parish
	m/d. 1814-1875	
Tullow	b/d. 1863-	None survive
Ward	See Finglas	
Westpalstown (with Clonmethan)		None survive
Whitechurch	b/m/d. 1824-1877	Local parish
St Mary (Donnybrook)	b/m/d. 1712-1870	Local parish

In addition to these, the records of some Army Chapels are held at the RCB Library. These are Richmond Barracks (b. 1857-72); Portobello Barracks (b. 1857-69); Pigeon House Fort (b. 1873-1901); Beggars Bush Barracks (1868-1921) and Arbour Hill Barracks (b. 1848-1922; m. 1847-1884).

From 1806 to 1837 the Rev. J.G. Schulze conducted marriage ceremonies (and a few baptisms) at his Dublin Church. These 4000 marriages were unwitnessed but were subsequently declared legal in court proceedings. The records are held at the Registrar General's Office (see p. 81).

4.3 Records of Other Denominations

Presbyterian records generally do not begin until after 1819, from which year Presbyterian ministers were required to keep records. However, because marriages in Presbyterian churches or kirks were not recognized until 1845, many Presbyterian marriages took place in the Church of Ireland and these records should therefore be consulted. Presbyterian churches rarely kept burial records.

Presbyterian Records

Abbey Church, Abbey St	1777
Ormond Quay	1787
Clontarf	1836

Huguenot Records

There were 2 "waves" of Huguenot arrivals in Ireland, the first being in the mid 17th century and the second in the early 18th. Both groups established their own churches. The major Huguenot churches were at St. Mary's Chapel in St Patrick's Cathedral, St Mary's Abbey, Wood Street and Lucy Lane. The full records of these churches were destroyed in the Public Record Office fire of 1922. However, records of the four Huguenot churches which existed in Dublin from 1680 to 1830 had previously been printed in volumes 7 and 14 of the publications of the Huguenot Society of London.

Quaker Records

All available Quaker meeting house records are preserved in the Religious Society of Friends Historical Library, Swanbrook House, Morehampton Road, , Dublin 4.

Jewish Records

The first Jewish synagogue in Ireland was in St Mary's Abbey. This was moved to Adelaide Road in 1892. Birth and death records prior to 1870 are held at the Irish Jewish Museum, 3/4 Walworth Road, South Circular Road, Dublin 8 in which many other relevant documents and artefacts are also held. More recent records, including marriage records, are held in the current synagogues at Adelaide Road, Leicester Avenue, Dublin 6, and Terenure.

There are 2 relevant accounts of Irish Jews available: Louis Hyman, **A History of the Jews of Ireland,** London/Jerusalem, 1972: and B. Schillmans, **Short History of the Jews of Ireland**, Dublin, 1945.

1834 first Feb 212

February first John Dunne Mrs Ellie Bonyuge.

Feb. first Christopher Sparks & Rosanna Kennedy.

Feb. Thomas Donnely & Anne Butler

Feb. 2 Richard Taylor & Eliza Andrew

Feb. 2 Thomas Gavenagh & Anne Karvin.

Feb. 3 William Howe & Eliza McMullen. —

Feb. 3 Edward Ellis & Jane Leslie

Feb. 4 John Tuke & Mary Walsh.

Feb. 4 Patrick McCabe & Catherin Lee.

Feb. 4 Michael Lawlor Charlotte Farroll.

Feb. 4 Richard Moore & Julia Byrne.

Feb. 4 George Brien & Ester Crannely.

Feb. 5 Thomas Healy & Margaret Harigan.

Feb. 5 James While & Mary A. Brader

Feb. 6 Mathew Noble & Eliza Smith.

Feb. 8 Michael Charls Price 14 Kings light Dr. Mary. England

Feb. 7 Wm Houldsworth P. 12 Reg Lanc. Bridget McDermoth

Feb. 8 Edward Ruthven Wright Esq. Miss Elizabeth Bateman

Feb. 8 Abraham Fagerty & Ester Gannon.

Feb. 8 Mr Nathaniel Hunt & Miss Amilia Goodison

Extract from the marriage register of the Rev Schulze, a Lutheran Minister, who performed marriages at the German Church, Poolbeg St, Dublin from 1806 to 1837.

CHAPTER 5

Commercial and Local Directories

Dublin has a good selection of commercial directories. These list the various tradesmen, professionals, gentry and, in some cases, inhabitants of Dublin city and the other towns and villages in the county.

The most comprehensive national directories were Pigot's *Commercial Directory of Ireland* of 1820 and 1824, and Slater's *Royal National Commercial Directory of Ireland* of 1846, '56, '70 and '81. These cover Dublin and most large towns in the county. There are also many local directories, some of which are excellent with detailed lists of occupants by street. Others will only list the more prominent citizens. Most directories include lists of local public officials, magistrates and gentry. They almost always have a list of tradesmen. Some of the better directories also include a house-by-house list of occupants on each street, and are therefore very valuable in locating urban-dwellers. In some cases the directories also list the major farmers in the immediate vicinity of the town.

Directories are particularly good for Dublin City. There are annual directories from 1755 to the present day. From 1755 to 1815 *The Treble Almanack* included only merchants and traders, from then to 1834 it contained nobility and gentry as well. In that year Pettigrew and Oulton's *Dublin Almanac* began with a house-to-house listing of the main streets, and from the following year it also contained an alphabetical list of individuals. This directory ceased publication in 1849 but in the meantime Thom's Directory had begun. This contained all of the lists in Pettigrew and Oulton's and other additional information. It has been published every year up to the present day.

These directories are available in several Dublin Libraries, including the National Library of Ireland and Trinity College Dublin.

1751   Wilson's *Alphabetical list of Names and Places of Abode of the Merchants and Traders of the City of Dublin.*

1752   Similar list published as supplement to *Gentleman's & Citizen's Almanac*. Further edition in 1753.

WILSON'S

Dublin Directory

FOR THE YEAR 1832,

BEING THE

SECOND YEAR OF WILLIAM IV.

FROM JUNE 1830,

AND

THE THIRTY-SECOND YEAR OF THE UNION OF GREAT BRITAIN AND IRELAND;

CONTAINING

AN ALPHABETICAL LIST OF THE MERCHANTS, TRADERS, JUDGES, BARRISTERS, ATTORNIES, SOLICITORS, ADVOCATES, PROCTORS, PUBLIC-NOTARIES, PHYSICIANS, SURGEONS, &c.

AND A NEW LIST OF THE NOBILITY AND GENTRY

Their Town and Country Residences, &c. &c.

To which is annexed, a NEW PLAN OF DUBLIN, and a LIST of STREETS, which mutually explain and illustrate each other.

ROYAL EXCHANGE.

DUBLIN:

PRINTED FOR THE PROPRIETOR, BY WM. FOLDS,
59, *Great Strand-street.*

Price, 2s. 6d. Stamp Duty, 6d.

Title page of Wilson's Dublin Directory of 1832.

1755   Merchants and traders list in Ge*ntlemans & Citizens Almanac*
and   (renamed the *Treble Almanac* in 1787). Lists of Lawyers and
annually   medical practitioners were also added and lists of city officials,
to 1837   faculty of the College of Surgeons and physicians, clergy and
           city guild officers. In 1815 a list of nobility and gentry was
           added and was gradually enlarged from then on.

1820   J. Pigot's *Commercial Directory of Ireland* contains
           information on the gentry, nobility and traders in and around
           Dublin.

1824   J. Pigot's *City of Dublin & Hibernian Provincial Directory*
           includes traders, nobility, gentry and clergy lists of Dublin,
           Howth, Lucan and Swords.

1834   Pettigrew & Oulton's *Dublin Almanac & General Register of*
and   *Ireland* has lists of merchants and traders, and of various other
annually   categories. It also has a list of residents of each of the main
to 1849   streets. The residents of rented houses, of which there were
           many, were generally not listed, these premises being referred
           to as tenements. The scope of the directory was gradually
           increased over the years to include the suburbs.

1844 and   Alexander Thom's *Irish Almanac & Official Directory* has the
annually   same categories of lists as Pettigrew & Oulton. It expanded
to date   rapidly to include the Dublin suburbs

1846   Slater's *National Commercial Directory of Irela*nd lists
           nobility, clergy, traders etc. in Balbriggan and Skerries,
           Blackrock, Booterstown, Dalkey, Dublin, Howth, Kingstown
           (Dun Laoghaire), Monkstown, Swords, Malahide and
           Williamstown.

1850   Henry Shaw's *New City Pictorial Directory of Dublin City* has
           a list of residents of the main streets, an alphabetical list of
           residents, and lists of attornies and barristers. It also has
           interesting line drawings of the street fronts showing shop
           names etc.

1856   Slater's R*oyal National Commercial Directory of Ireland* lists
           nobility, gentry, clergy, traders etc. in; Balbriggan and Skerries,
           Dublin and Kingstown (Dun Laoghaire), Howth, Swords and
           Malahide.

1870   Slater's *Directory of Ireland* contains trade, nobility and clergy

NOBILITY AND GENTRY.

Note.—The private Residents of the Professional and Trading Classes will be found under their respective heads.

Achmuty (Mrs. S.) 23, *Rutland-str.*
Acton (Miss M.) 77, *Stephen's-gr. S.*
Adáir (Mrs.) 64, *Mount-street,* and *Belgrove, Monasterevan.*
Adams (Mrs. Isabella) 2, *Russell-st.*
Adams (Sam. esq.) 45, *Eccles-street.*
Adamson (J. esq.) 55, *Aungier-str.*
Adamson (Rev. A.S.) 14, *Blackhall-st.*
Agar (Wm. esq.) 4, *Molesworth-str.*
Airey (Maj. Gen.) 14, *Merr.-sq. N.*
Alexander (Robert, sen. esq.) 12, *Merrion-square,* and *Seapoint.*
Alexander (Sir Wm.) *Booterstown.*
Alexander (W.J.esq.)16,*Fitz-sq.W.*
Alexander (W. esq.) 4, *up. Baggot-s.*
Alexander (W. esq.) 1, *Richmond-pl.*
Allen (Captain) 3, *Richmond-street.*
Allen (Edm. esq.) 3, *low. Fitzw.-str.*
Allen (Lieu.Col.) 36, *l. Gardiner's-s.*
Allen (Lord Viscount) 10, *Merrion-square, S.*
Allen (Rich. esq.) 24, *Eccles-street.*
Anderson (E.esq.) 33,*up.Gloucester-s.*
Anderson (Mrs.) 15, *Charlemont-st.*
Anderson (Mrs.) 18, *Mount-street.*
Anderson (Mrs. M.) 12, *Cuffe-str.*
Anderson (Mrs.) 148, *Mecklb.-str.*
Anderson (Rob. esq.) 22, *Brunsw.-s.*
Annesley (Hon.Fra.) 29, *Molesw.-st.*
Annesley (Rev. Mr.) 2, *S. Cumb.-s.*
Anson (Hon. G.) 3d Guards, *Dublin Castle.*
Arabin (Henry, esq.) 12, *Clare-str.* and *Corka, Clondalkin.*
Archbold (Miss E.) 39, *Gloucester-st.*
Archdall (John, esq.) *Merrion-str.*
Archdall (Hon.Mrs.M) 1,*Kildare-p. Castle Archdall, Co. Fermanagh.*
Archer (Ald.) 9, *Gardiner's-place.*
Archer (Mrs.) 65, *Stephen's-gr. S.*
Archer (John esq.) *North-wall.*
Ardagh (Dean of) 26, *Harcourt-st.*

Armagh (Archd. of) 7, *Mer.-sq. E.* and *Aughnacloy.*
Armit (John,esq.) 1, *Kildare-street,* and *Newtown-park.*
Armitage (Mrs.) 45, *Bishop-street.*
Armstrong (Capt.) 17, *Prussia-str.*
Armstrong (Col.) 73, *Mount-street.*
Armstrong (Colonel) *Merrion-str.*
Armstrong (E. esq.)51, *Dominick-st*
Armstrong (Mrs. D.) 12,*l. Dorset-st*
Armstrong (Mrs.) 43, *up. Rutl.-str.*
Armstrong (Rev. Mr.)32,*Hardw.-st.*
Armstrong (R. esq.) *up. Baggot-str.*
Armstrong (Tho. esq.) 41, *Bless.-st.*
Arnold (Jas. esq.) 45, *up. Rutland-st.* and *Banbridge, Co. Down.*
Arran (Dowager Countess of) 21, *Kildare-street.*
Arthure (B. esq.) 42, *Dominick-str.*
Arthure (Mrs.) 8, *Charlemont-str.*
Arthure (Mrs. J.) 9, *Gloucester-str.*
Ashe (Major) 4, *up. Rutland-street.*
Ashe (Mrs.) 24, *Mount-street.*
Ashe (Mrs. W.) 45, *Leeson-street.*
Ashworth (J. esq.) 5, *S. Cumb.-str.*
Ashworth (R. esq.) 16, *Mer.-sq. N.*
Atkinson (John, esq.) 1, *Ely-place.*
Atkinson(John,esq.)3,*Blessington-st.*
Atkinson (Jos. esq.) 34, *gt. Ship-st.*
Attorney-General (Rt. Hon. the) 27, *Steph.-gr. N.*&*Carysfort-park.*
Austin (Colonel) *Dublin Castle.*
Aylmer (Lord) *Royal Hospital.*
Aylmer (Mrs. Cath.) 1, *Eccles-str.*
Aylmer (Mrs. E.) 24, *Queen-street.*
Aylward (Nich. esq.) 9, *Temple-str.* and *Shankhill Castle, Co. Kilkenny.*

B.

Babington(Mrs.T.)14,*Blessington-s.*
Bacon (James C.esq.) 27,*Temple-str.*
Bacon (Miss S.) 8, *gt. Ship-street.*
Bagot (Mrs. D.) 36, *Leeson-street.*

lists for Balbriggan and Skerries, Dalkey, Dublin, Dundrum, Howth, Rathfarnham, Swords and Malahide.

1881   Slater's *Royal National Commercial Directory of Ireland* contains lists of traders, clergy, nobility and farmers in adjoining parishes of the towns of Balbriggan and Skerries, Donabate and Malahide, Dublin, Howth and Baldoyle, Rathfarnham and Swords.

1894   Slater's *Royal National Directory of Ireland* lists traders, police, teachers, farmers and private residents in Dublin City and in each of the towns, villages and parishes of the county.

28 to 39 Jacob and Co. W. R. (ltd.),
14*l.*, 10*l.*, 16*l.*, 14*l.*
40 & 41 Tonge and Taggart, *South City* foundry and iron works, 52*l.*
42 to 44 Tenements, 14*l.* to 17*l.*
45 Tenements, 39*l.*
46 Jacob, W. R. and Co. (limited) . .
.........*here Bishop-court intersects.........*
47 to 49 Tenements, 20*l.* 9*l.*
50 Adams, Stephen, contractor, and 4 to 7 Peter-street, and 39 Stephen's-green—res. 78 Circular-rd. sth. 30*l.*
51 Vacant, 18*l.*
52, 53 to 55 Tenements, 22*l.*, 23*l.*
54 & 55 Tenements, 17*l.*, 16*l.*
56 Leigh, P. provision merchant, 21*l.*

3 N.—Blackhall-parade.

From Blackhall-street to King-street, Nth. P. St. Paul.—Arran-quay W.

1 Finegan, Miss, dressmaker, 9*l.*
2 Smith, Mrs. lodgings, 9*l.*
3 Murphy, Mrs. M. 13*l.*
4 Condron, J. horseshoer and far. 4*l.*
5, 6 & 7 Millner, Robt. & Sons, wool stores, with 55 Queen-street
8 Davis, Mr. M. 15*l.*
9 Clarke, Joseph, watch maker, 11*l.*
10 Tenements
11 Duignan, Mrs. 14*l.*

3 N.—Blackhall-place.

From Ellis's-quay to Stoneybatter. P. St. Paul.—Arran-quay W.

KING'S, OR BLUE COAT HOSPITAL—George R. Armstrong, esq. agent and registrar; Rev. T. B. Gibson, chaplain and schoolmaster
1 and 2 Menton, Denis, dairy, and 17 King-street, north, 92*l.*, 30*l.*
3 and 4 Losty, Mr. M. J. 30*l.*, 34*l.*
5 Watson, Mr. William T.
6 and 7 Paul and Vincent, farming implement manufs. millwrights, and iron founders, chemical manure and vitriol manufacturers, and Rogerson's-quay, 33*l.*
8 Rice, A. stone & marble works, 14*l.*
9 Moran, James, axle tree manufacturer, 24*l.*
here Stoneybatter and King-street, North, intersect.
10 to 14 Tenements, 12*l.*
15 O'Haire, Matthew, hide & rag merchant, 18*l.*
16 Vacant, 15*l.*
17 Tenements, 5*l.*
18 Flanigan, Mrs. 5*l.*
19 Vacant,
.........*here Blackhall-street intersects.......*

3 Gordon, Samuel, wholesale brush manufacturer, 18*l.*
4 *The National Hotel*—M. A. Meaney, proprietress, 26*l.*
5 Baird, Jas. A. surg., L.R.C.S.I. 27*l.*
6 Tenements, 27*l.*
7 Dillon, Mr. John, 27*l.*
8 Torney, Thomas, M.D. M.R.C.S.E. M.R.C.P.I. 37*l.*
9 and 10 Tenements, 30*l.*, 32*l.*
11 Vacant, 25*l.*
12 and 13 Tenements, 25*l.*, 24*l.*
14 MacNeil, John Gordon Swift, M.A. OXON. barrister, M.P. 26*l.*
15 Tenements, 29*l.*
.........*here Blackhall-place intersects.......*
16 to 18 Fitzgerald, P. corn and seed stores, 10*l.* 12*l.* 12*l.*
19 & 20 Hickey & Co. stores office, 10*l.*
21 Martin, Mrs. E. 21*l.*
22 and 23 Tenements, each 21*l.*
24 Tenements
25 to 27 Tenements, 21*l.*, 22*l.*, 22*l.*
28 Tenements, 23*l.*
29 Hickey, Paul, & Co. cattle salesmrs. corn, hay, and wool factors, 24*l.*
30 Tenements, 21*l.*
31 and 32 Tenements, each 20*l.*

3 S.—Blackpitts.

From New-row, South, to Greenville-av. P. St. Nicholas Without, east side. P. St. Luke, west.—Merchants'-quay W.
.......*here Funbally's-lane intersects.......*
1 Tenements, 8*l.*
2 Tenements, 4*l.*
Corporation depot
.........*here Malpas-street intersects.........*
12 Geoghegan, H., dairy, 4*l.* 10*s.*
13 Kinsella, Mr. P.
14 to 21 Small cottages
here Roper's-rest & Donovan's-lane inters.
Here Artisans' Dwellings, 120 houses, intersect.
22 Hendrick, Mr. Andrew
23 Tenements, 20*l.*
24 Tenements, 6*l.*
25 Murphy, T. dairy, 18*l.*
26 Smyth, Samuel, 6*l.*
27 Malone, Mr. James, 15*l.*
27½ Healy, J. car and float owner
28 Ryan, Mary, manuf. chemist, 35*l.*
29 Tenements
30 Vacant,
32 Fleming, Robert, dairy, 8*l.*
33 Tenements, 9*l.*
34 Doyle, Mr., 9*l.*
35 Sheehan, Mr Richard, 3*l.*
36 Scully, Mr. Thomas, 3*l.*
37 Horan, Mr. James, 3*l.*

Sample page from the Dublin Street Directory in Thom's Official Directory, 1893.

150   *Barristers.*

BARRISTERS at LAW, *with the* DATES *of their* ADMISSION.

Note. The Letters H [*Hilary*] E [*Easter*] T [*Trinity*] and M [*Michael-mas*] shew the Terms, and the Figures, the years, in which they were called to the Bar. K. C. denotes King's Council ; and M. P. Member of Parliament.   Where the town residence is not mentioned, the omission is owing, in some cases, to the want of information, which the practising Barristers are requested to supply.

☞ Thus marked § were called to the English Bar.

A.

Admission.
M. 1806 Abbot (John)
E. 1796 Adair (H.) 6, *Mountjoy-p.*
T. 1785 Alexander (H.)
H. 1794 Allen (C.E.) 3, *Fitzwm.-st.*
E. 1812 Allen (Hen. F.) 26, *Beres-ford-street.*
H. 1793 Alley (Peter)
M. 1798 Anderson (Edw.) 30, *up. Gloucester-street.*
M. 1792 Anderson (R.) 17, *Digges-s*
T. 1770 Annesley (Rt. Hon. R. Earl) *Castlewellan.*
H. 1796 Antisell (C.) 61, *Gardiner-s*
H. 1775 Apjohn (Mich. Marshall)
T. 1803 Arabin (Hen. Wm.)
M. 1799 §Archdale (Richard)
E. 1814 Archer (H.B.) 65, *Steph.-g.*
M. 1814 Ardill (J.W.) 74 *Aungier-s.*
H. 1779 Armstrong (E.)
M. 1819. Armstrong (Wm.) 20, *low. Ormond-quay.*
E. 1804 Arthure (J.) 3, *Mountjoy-s.*
E. 1814 Arthure (P E.)
T. 1785 Atkinson (J.T.) *Hume-st.*
E. 1795 Atkinson (J. Wray)

B.

E. 1800 Baker (R.) 105, *Summer-h.*
H. 1792 Baker (William)
M. 1788 Baker (Wm. Jephson)
H. 1798 Baldwin (Richard)
M. 1780 Ball (Benj.) *Merrion-sq. S.*
H. 1781 Ball (Chas.) 26, *Temple-st.*
H. 1795 Ball (J.) Com. of Bankr. 16, *up. Gardiner-street.*
M. 1774 Ball (James)
H. 1815 Ball John) 3, *l. Pemb.-str.*
M. 1814 Ball (N.) 16, *Mt.joy-sq. N.*
E. 1800 Ball (Thomas) Master in Chancery, L.L.D.

Admission.
E. 1775 Ball (W.) L.L.D. 7, *Clare-street.*
T. 1815 Barber (Jn.) 31, *Harcourt-s.*
M. 1816 Barlow (J.) *N. gt. Geo.-str.*
E. 1787 Barrett (Rog.) *Montague-s.*
T. 1787 Barrington (Sir Jonah) K. C. Judge Adm. Court.
E. 1791 Barry (Jos.)
M. 1811 Barry (G.S.) 6, *l. Mer.-st*
H. 1802 Barry (T.) 4, *l. Merrion-st*
M. 1785 Barry (W.N.) 54, *Granby-r*
H. 1788 Barwick (William)
E. 1816 Barwis (John)
H. 1788 Bateman (Geo. Brooke)
H. 1780 Bateman (J.) 49, *Castle-st*
T. 1798 Battersby (William)
T. 1791 Battley (T. C) 4, *Baggot-s.*
T. 1781 Batty (J. E.)
T. 1788 Bayly (John) *Dorset-street*
M. 1818 Beamish (Robert)
E. 1802 Beatty (F.) 7, *Mountjoy-square, S.*
T. 1810 Beatty (T.) 100, *Baggot-st*
T. 1788 Beauman (Ch.)
T. 1789 Bell (J.W.) 1, *Gardiner-st*
H. 1811 Bell (Thos.) 3, *Hatch-str.*
T. 1791 Bellew (William) 10, *gt. Charles-street.* ·
E. 1800 Bennett (G.) 1, *Fitzwm.-s.*
H. 1796 Bennett (R.N.) 23, *Harc.-st*
H. 1808 Bennett (R.) 26, *Molesw.-st*
M. 1793 Benson (C.) Commis. of Bankr. *Baggot-street.*
M. 1806 Bessonet (Js.) Assist. Bar. Co. Carlow, 27, *Leeson-s.*
M. 1818 Betty (James)
E. 1776 Betty (W.) L. L. D. 32, *Rutland-square, W.*
E. 1794 Bethell (I. B.)
T. 1805 Blackburne (F) 10, *Leinst.-s*

A listing of Dublin Barristers from "Wilsons' Dublin Directory for the year 1832".

CHAPTER 6

Newspapers

The earliest known Irish newspaper was published in 1649. During the 18th century the numbers increased greatly and by the 19th century most large towns had at least one and some towns had several. By 1900 Dublin had seen the publication of some 70 different newspaper titles.

Announcements of marriages, deaths and births are the most obvious items of interest in these newspapers. However these mainly occur after the mid 18th century. Individual papers differed in their policy to advertisements, some contained many, others less. The policy also changed over the lives of some newspapers. Birth, marriage and death notices, as might be expected, usually refer to the middle and upper classes. The birth notices tend to be less valuable since the name of the child and even the mother is usually not given. Birth notices often take the form "At Lucan, the wife of John Byrne Esq, of a daughter". There was a widespread practice of city newspapers repeating the notices appearing in provincial newspapers, often in an abridged form. If a notice of a rural "event" is found in a city newspaper, it is usually wise to check some of the local papers as more details may be found.

Basic news items are rarely of interest since names are not frequent, other than in court cases. Advertisements are an important source of information for tradesmen and other businessmen. These are common in most newspapers.

Arguably the best Dublin newspapers for the 18th century are Faulkner's Dublin Journal, the Freeman's Journal, Dublin Hibernian Journal, and the Dublin Evening Post. In the 19th century further useful papers began publication including the Dublin Morning Post, Dublin Evening Herald and Dublin Evening Mail. A card index to biographical notices in Faulkner's Dublin Journal from 1763-1771 is held in the National Library of Ireland.

In this guide the main newspapers for the city and county are listed. Also listed are the holdings of each paper in the National Library of Ireland which has one of the best collections of Irish newspapers, and in the British Library. The holdings are listed according to the month and year beginning and ending each series, eg 4.1849-5.1853 is April 1849 to May 1953. Listing of the year only indicates that the full year's issues are held.

Title: **Constitution and Church Sentinel**
Published in: Dublin: 1849-1853
BL Holdings: 4.1849-5.1853

Title: **Dublin Courant**
Published in: Dublin: 1702-1725; new series 1744-1750
NLI Holdings: odd nos. 1703, 1705; 6.1744-2.1752; many
                   issues missing.
BL Holdings: odd nos 1718, '19, '20, '22, 1.1723-12.1725;
                   4.1744-3.1750

Title: **Correspondent**
Published in: Dublin: 1806-1861
Note: Called Dublin Correspondent in 1822;
                   Evening Packet and Correspondent in 1828;
                   Evening Packet in 1860
NLI Holdings: 11.1806-12.1861
BL Holdings: 11.1806-4.1810; odd nos 1810, 11, 13, 14, 15,
                   16 & 20;1-12.1823; odd nos 1825, 26

Title: **Dublin Chronicle**
Published in: Dublin: 1762-1817
Note: Breaks in Publication
NLI Holdings: 1.1770-12.1771; 5.1787-12.1793;
                   6.1815-1817 (odd nos)
BL Holdings: 5.1787-4.1792; 5-12.1793

Title: **Dublin Evening Mail**
                   (Continued as Evening Mail)
Published in: Dublin: 1823-1962
NLI Holdings: 2.1823-7.1962
BL Holdings: 2.1823-2.1928

Title: **Dublin Evening Post**
Published in: Dublin: 1732-1737; 1778-1875
NLI Holdings: 6.1732-1.1737; 2.1778-8.1875
BL Holdings: 6.1732-7.1734; 7.1737-7.1741; 8.1778-7.1753;

10.1783-12.1785; 1787; 1789; 1792; 1794;
5-6.1795; 1.1796-12.1797; 1.1804-12.1810;
odd nos 1813 & 14; 1.1815-8.1875

Title:	**Dublin Gazette**
	(Continued as Iris Oifiguil in 1922)
Published in:	Dublin: 1705-current
Note:	(Government notices)
NLI Holdings:	11.1706-12.1727; 3.1729-4.1744; 6.1756-12.1759,
	1760, 1762, 1763, 1765,
	1766, 1767, 1-7.1775; 1776-1788; 1790-1921

Title:	**Dublin Gazette (Weekly Courant)**
Published in:	Dublin: 1703-1728
NLI Holdings:	odd nos. 1708

Title:	**Dublin Intelligence**
Published in:	Dublin: 1690-1767 (at various times under different
	managements)
NLI Holdings:	9.1690-5.1693; 6.1702-11.1731
BL Holdings:	odd nos 1708-1712 and 1723-1725

Title:	**Dublin Journal —**
	See **Faulkner's Dublin Journal**

Title:	**Dublin Mercury**
	(Continued as **Hoey's Dublin Mercury**
	in 1770)
Published in:	Dublin: 1704-1775
NLI Holdings:	12.1722-5.1724; 1-9.1726; 1-9.1742;
	9.1770-4.1773
BL Holdings:	1-9.1742; 3.1766-4.1773

Title:	**Dublin Morning Post**
	(Published as **Carrick's Morning Post**
	in 1804-1821)
Published in:	Dublin: c1804-1832
NLI Holdings:	4.1814-1831
BL Holdings:	odd nos 1824-26; 1.1830-5.1832

Title: **Evening Freeman**
Published in: Dublin: 1831-1871
NLI Holdings: 8.1831-7.1836; 4-12.1844; 1845-9.1847;
odd nos. 1848; 2.1858-1859
BL Holdings: 1.1831-6.1871

Title: **Evening Irish Times**
Published in: Dublin: c1860-1921
NLI Holdings: 4.1896-3.1900; 7.1900-3.1901; 7.1901-1907;
1911-6.1915
BL Holdings: 10.1880-10.1921

DUBLIN—MARCH 20, 1813.

MELANCHOLY ACCIDENT.

On Thursday, about two o'clock in the afternoon, a waiter belonging to the Carlisle Tavern, of the name of William Bryan, was proceeding aboard one of the Carlingford boats, lying at the slip, at Carlisle-bridge, when he was suddenly seized with an epileptic fit, and fell into the river ; twenty minutes elapsed before the body was taken up ; it was brought to the Dispensary in Temple-bar, when the usual means used by the Humane Society was resorted to, but in vain, as the vital spark was extinct—the unfortunate man has left a widow and five helpless children to lament his loss.

Title: **Evening Herald**
Published in: Dublin: 1786-1814; new series 1891-in progress
NLI Holdings: 5.1786-12.1789; 1.1806-12.1809;
odd nos. 1810; 1.1812-6.1814
BL Holdings: 5.1786-12.1789; odd nos 1807; 1813; 12.1891-

Title: **Evening Packet** (incorporated
with **Dublin Evening Mail**)
Published in: Dublin: 1828-1862
BL Holdings: 1.1828-4.1929; 9.1829-3.1862

Title: **Evening Telegraph**
Published in: Dublin: 1871-1924

NLI Holdings:	10.1884-12.1924
BL Holdings:	7.1871-11.1873; 8.1875-5.1916; 1.1919-12.1924

Title: **Faulkner's Dublin Journal**
Published in: Dublin: 1725-1825
NLI Holdings: 1.1726-7.1735; 5.1736-1782; 1787-1790; 1.1791-4.1825
BL Holdings: odd nos 1726, 39, 40; 3.1741; 8-12.1744; 3.1748-3.1750; 3.1751-12.1764; 12.1765-12.1768; odd nos 1782-1784, 1792; 1-12.1796; odd nos 1798, 99, 1803; 10.1804-12.1810 odd nos 1813, 14, 17; 12.1819-12.1821

Title: **Freeman's Journal or Public Register**
Published in: Dublin: 1763-1924
NLI Holdings: 9.1763-12.1924
BL Holdings: odd nos 1763-1767; 9.1767-9.1775; 12.1775-6.1777; odd nos 1779-1780; 9.1782-6.1783; 11.1783-12.1784; odd nos 1823, '24; 1.1830-12.1833; 1.1837-12.1924

Title: **General Advertiser**
Published as: Dublin: 1804-1924
NLI Holdings: 9.1804-11.1820; odd nos. 1837; 2.1841-12.1851; 1853, 1854, 1857-61; 1864; 1866, 1867, 1869, 1870, 1874- 12.1877; 1.1880-1890; 1892-3.1924
BL Holdings: 10.1838-12.1840; (with gaps); odd nos 1841 & 1846; 12.1846-7.1914; 1.1915-12.1923

Title: **Impartial Occurences**
(Continued as **Peu's Occurences** in 1714)
Published in: Dublin: 1704-1780
NLI Holdings: 12.1704-2.1706; 12.1718-1748; 1751-1755; 1.1756-5.1757 4-12.1768
BL Holdings: 1.1705-2.1706; odd nos 1714, 1719, 1740; 1.1741-12.1742; 1.1744-12.1749; 1.1752-12.1753; 1.1756-12.1758; 1761

BIRTHS.

At Upper Buckingham-street, on the 1st instant, the lady of George D. Plomer, Esq., of a daughter.

June 1, at 154, Great Britain-street, the lady of Thomas Birmingham Trotter, Esq., of a daughter, which survived only a few hours.

On the 31st instant, at Ballyward Lodge, county Down, the lady of Francis C. Beers, Esq., of a son and heir.

On the 30th instant, at No. 11, Middle Gardiner-street, the lady of Captain F. S. Jones, of a son and heir.

DIED,

On the 25th of May, at Bushy Park, county of Wicklow, the Hon. and Rev. Boleyn Howard, uncle to the Earl of Wicklow.

On the 30th ult., at Clontarf, whither he had retired for the benefit of his health, Mr. William Dalton, for upwards of thirty years Master of the King's Hospital, the duties of which office he always discharged with zeal, fidelity and efficiency, so as to merit for him the approbation of the Governors of the Institution, and the lasting gratitude of his numerous pupils.

THEATRE ROYAL, DUBLIN.

First appearance these three years of Mr. and Mrs. YATES—First appearance of Monsieur BIHIN, the Belgian Giant—And also of the original troupe of Parisian MONKEYS.

THIS EVENING (Monday), June 3, the Entertainments will commence with the Domestic Drama of
VICTORINE;
Or, I'll Sleep on it.
In which Mr. and Mrs. Yates will appear.
After which the Performances of the celebrated
PARISIAN MONKEYS.
The Entertainments will conclude with the new Cambrian Legendary Drama called the
GIANT'S CASTLE;
Or, The Well of Marble Waters.
In which Mons. Bihin will appear.

Notices from "Saunder's Newsletter & Daily Advertiser" of June 3, 1839.

Title:	**The Irish Times**
Published in:	Dublin: 1859-current
Note:	Evening and Weekly versions listed under **Evening IrishTimes** and **Weekly Irish Times**
NLI Holdings:	3.1859-in progress
BL Holdings:	3.1859-in progress (except part of 11.1871)

Title:	**Kingstown Gazette**
Published in:	Kingstown (Dun Laoghaire): old series 1857-1858; NS. 1868-1869
BL Holdings:	12.1857-1.1858; 5.1868-7.1869

Title:	**Magee's Weekly Packet**
Published in:	Dublin: 1777-1793
NLI Holdings:	6.1777-3.1895; 3.1787-8.1790; 8.1792-8.1793
BL Holdings:	6.1777-10.1777; 11.1777-3.1785; odd nos to 1793

Title:	**Morning Mail**
Published in:	Dublin: 1870-1912
NLI Holdings:	2.1870-12.1883
BL Holdings:	3.1871-6.1880; 12.1896-8.1912 (with gaps)

Title:	**Morning Register**
Published in:	Dublin: 1824-1843
NLI Holdings:	10.1824-1.1843
BL Holdings:	10.1824-1.1843

Title:	**Nation** (Continued as (1) Daily Nation (2) Weekly Nation)
Published in:	Dublin: 1842-1900
NLI Holdings:	10.1842-7.1891; 6.1896-9.1900
BL Holdings:	10.1824-7.1848; 9.1849-7.1891; 6.1896-9.1900

Title:	**Patriot** (Continued as Statesman and Patriot in 1828)
Published in:	Dublin: c1810-1829
NLI Holdings:	7.1810-1815; 1818-10.1828; 11.1829-5.1829
BL Holdings:	1.1823-10.1828

TYD—E

Business notices from the Irish Times of March 31, 1898.

Title: **Saunder's Newsletter**
                           (Continued as **Saunder's Irish Daily News**
                           in 1878)
Published in: Dublin: 1755-1879
NLI Holdings: Odd nos. 1767-1791; 3.1773-12.1787;
                           1.1789-3.1795; 2.1796-12.1802;
                           4.1804-12.1806; 1.1808-11.1809; 1812-1818;
                           1820-11.1879
BL Holdings: 3.1773-12.1787; 1789; 1.1793-12.1794; 1795;
                           1.1797-12.1811; 1.1813-12.1815;
                           1.1817-11.1879

Title: **The Warder**
                           (Continued as **Sport's Mail** and
                           Irish Weekly Mail in 1921)
Published in: Dublin: 1821-1939
NLI Holdings: 3.1821-9.1938
BL Holdings: 3.1822-9.1939 (except 1930)

Title: **Weekly Freeman's Journal**
Published in: Dublin: c1817-1924
Note: Continued as **Weekly Freeman, National Press**
                           and **Irish Agriculturist** (Dublin) in 1892
NLI Holdings: 1-7.1818; 3-7.1830; 1.1834-4.1840;
                           6.1880-12.1882; 5.1883-3.1892;
                           4.1892-12.1893; 1.1895-12.1913; 6.1914-
                           12.1924
BL Holdings: 10.1821-12.1831; 1.1838-3.1892;
                           4.1892-12.1924

Title: **Weekly Irish Times**
                           (Continued as **Times Pictorial** in 1941)
                         Published in: Dublin: 1875-1941
NLI Holdings: Odd nos. 1875; 1.1883-6.1886; 1.1906-11.1941
BL Holdings: 6.1875-12.1920; 1.1922-11.1941

CHAPTER 7

Family Histories

An ideal for many is to find that their ancestors have been described in detail by some previous researcher. Although this is rarely the case, the possibility always exists. Published histories generally deal with the more prominent families of Ireland and usually to the "gentry". The publications listed in this chapter are those which

(a) specifically refer to a family from one part of the city or county, or

(b) refer to families which are particularly linked with Dublin. There are many other references to specific families in local history publications and other general sources (see p. 84).

Acton Papers (Stradbrook, Co. Dublin) Anal.Hib. 25, 3-13.

Arnoldi of Dublin, 27 entries in the family Bible. J. Ass. Pres. Mem. Dead, Vol. VIII, 1910-1912, p. 71.

Ashe see *Cooke*

Barnewall Ir. Gen. 5(2) 1975, 181-185.

The *Barnewalls* of Turvey. Reportorium Novum 1(2) 1956, p. 336-341.

Bath family Pedigree (Cappock Co Dublin) GO MS 163, p. 30

The *Bathes* of Drumcondra. Reportorium Novum 1(2) 1956, p. 328-30.

The *Brocas* family, notable Dublin artists. University Review, 2(6) 1959, 17-25.

Papers of the *Campbell* family of Prospect House, Terenure 1820-1916. GO MS 114, p. 175

Notes on the *Cooke, Ashe* and *Swift* families, all of Dublin. Ass. Pres. Mem. Dead. Vol. IX, 1912-1916 p. 503.

Cusack family of Meath and Dublin. Ir. Gen. 5(3) 1976 pp. 298-313; 5(4) 1977 pp. 464-470; 5(5) 1978 pp. 591-600; 5(6) 1979 pp. 673-684; 6(2) 1981 pp. 130-153; 6(3) 1982 pp. 285-298.

Dix family of Dublin, entries from family Bible. J. Ass. Pres. Mem. Dead.

Vol XI, 1921-25, p. 490.

The *Dexters* of Dublin and Annfield, Co. Kildare. Ir. Anc. 2(1), 1970 p. 31-42.

Fagans of Feltrim, Reportorium Novum 2(1) 1958, p. 103-106

The *Falkiners* of Abbotstown, Co. Dublin. J. Kildare Arch Hist. Soc., 8 (1915-17), 331-63.

The *Fitz Rerys,* Welsh lords of Cloghran, Co. Dublin. J. Louth Arch. Soc. 5 (1921), 13-17.

The *Fitzwilliams* of Merrion. Reportorium Novum 2(1) 1958, p. 88-96.

Gamble Family Papers (1890-1905) PRO M 5534 (1-18).

King's printers. Notes on the family of *Grierson* of Dublin. Ir. Gen., 2 (1953), 303-37.

The *Hollywoods* of Artane. Reportorium Novum 1(2) 1956, p. 341-344.

A *Kingsbury* of Dublin. Pedigree in Swanzy notebooks, RCB Library, Dublin.

Law family of Dublin, pedigree. J. Ass. Pres. Mem. Dead., Vol. XI, 1921-25, p. 444.

The *Lawless* family. Reportorium Novum 1(2) 1956, p. 344-350.

The *Magees* of Belfast and Dublin by F.J. Bigger. Belfast, 1916.

Moore of Rutland Square, Dublin. Pedigree in Swanzy notebooks, RCB Library, Dublin.

A *Moorhouse* family of Dublin, Carlow and Kildare. Ir. Anc. 9(1) 1977, p. 15-18.

Nottinghams of Ballyowen. Reportorium Novum 1(2) 1956, p. 323-324.

Pemberton of Dublin. Ir. Anc. 11(1) 1979, p. 14-26.

The *Plunketts* of Dunsoghly. Reportorium Novum 1(2) 1956, p. 330-336.

Plunketts of Portmarnock. Reportorium Novum 2(1) 1958, p. 106-108.

An early Dublin candlemaker: history of the family of *Rathborne,* chandlers, Dublin. Dublin Hist. Record, 14 (1957), 66-73.

The *Scurlocks* of Rathcredan. Reportorium Novum 1(1) 1955, p. 79-80.

Segraves of Cabra. Reportorium Novum 1(2) 1956, p. 324-328.

Deeds relating to the *Shaw* family, Bushy Park, Terenure. NLI D11, 465-D11, 603

A genealogical history of the family of *Sirr* of Dublin, London, 1903.

Swift see *Cooke*

Talbot de Malahide. Reportorium Novum 2(1) 1958, p. 96-103.

The *Talbots* of Belgard. Reportorium Novum 1(1) 1955, p. 80-83.

Genealogical memoir of the family of *Talbot* of Malahide, Co. Dublin, 1829.

The Dublin *Tweedys:* the story of an Irish family 1650-1882. by Owen Tweedy, London 1956.

Genealogical history of the *Tyrrells* of Castleknock in Co. Dublin, Fertullagh in Co. Westmeath and now of Grane Castle, Co. Meath by J.H. Tyrrell, London 1904.

The *Tyrrells* of Castleknock. RSAI 76 (1946), 151-4. A

The *Wolverstons* of Stillorgan. Reportorium Novum 2(2) 1960, p. 243-245.

CHAPTER 8

Wills, Administrations and Marriage Licences

Wills are legal documents detailing the wishes of a deceased person as to division of their property. Administrations are legal documents setting out the decisions of a court as to division of the property of those who died without making a will.

8.1 Wills

These are a particularly valuable source of genealogical information. They can contain detailed information on relationships between many members of a family group, together with other information on the residences, occupations, history and circumstances of the family. They are therefore well worth finding if they exist.

Until 1858 the church was responsible for proving (i.e. establishing the validity) of wills. From the reformation until 1858 this meant that the Church of Ireland, as the "established" church, was responsible. Within each Church of Ireland diocese there was a Consistorial Court which proved wills of those who had been resident within the diocese and whose property was also within the diocese. If however, the testators property in another diocese was of more than £5 value, the will was proven by a Prerogative court which was the responsibility of the Archbishop of Armagh. Furthermore, if the testator had property in England the will was also proved in the English court at Canterbury and a copy proved in Armagh. In particulare, recent immigrants to Ireland may have retained property in England.

One of the circumstances in which a will might have been proved in the Prerogative court is if the testator had land which straddled the border of two dioceses. All of Dublin city and county, as well as much of the surrounding counties, are in the Diocese of Dublin. The other major circumstance in which a testator's will might be in the Prerogative court is if he/she was wealthy and therefore had property, or goods, elsewhere in the country.

Most of the actual will documents (of all types) were destroyed in the fire at the Public Record Office in 1922. The records which are now available are of 3 types:

(a) Wills: these are the wills which survived the PRO fire, copies and further wills which have been obtained since 1922, and wills deposited in other archives such as the PRO, Registry of Deeds, NLI etc. (see 8.4).

Quaker wills from Dublin and East Leinster are held in the Society of Friends Library, Dublin. (see p. 81)

(b) Will Abstracts: many local or family historians have examined the wills concerned with certain families or areas over the centuries. The notes on the contents of these wills, called Abstracts, are available in the PRO and/or in other libraries.

Depending on the purpose for which they were made the abstracts will vary in their detail. They will usually contain the testators name and address, date of will and probate, executors name and the names of the major beneficiaries. The relationship of beneficiaries to the testator is also often indicated. Major abstract collections include Betham's Abstracts of Prerogative wills (see p. 75); and Eustace's collection of abstracts of wills deposited at the Registry of Deeds. Lane-Poole Papers containing Dublin and Wicklow abstracts are held in the NLI (Ms. 5359).

(c) Will Indexes: the major set of indexes to Irish wills are the books used in the PRO as a guide to finding the wills among their collection. The indexes to 'Consistorial' wills survived the fire although some were damaged. These are in the PRO and are arranged alphabetically by family name and christian name and give the address, (in some cases occupation) and year of probate. The indexes to consistorial wills have been published in various places. The major source is the series of volumes edited by Gertrude Thrift and published by W.W. Phillimore (London) from 1909-1920. These have been reprinted by Baltimore Genealogical Publishing Co. (1970).

The indexes to wills in the diocese of Dublin and Glendalough (1536-1858) were published in the appendices to the 26th and 30th reports of the DKPRI of 1895 and 1899 respectively.

Prerogative will indexes are arranged alphabetically by testators name and also give the address, occupation and year of probate. They are in 2 series, up to 1810, and from 1811 to 1857. The first series has been published as **Index to the Prerogative Wills of Ireland 1538-1810** Ed by Sir Arthur Vicars (1897). This was reprinted by Baltimore Genealogical Publishing Co. in 1967. The indexes are also available in the PRO.

KEEPER OF THE PUBLIC RECORDS IN IRELAND. 213

Name, Place, and Occupation.	Year.	Nature of Record.	Page.
Dalton, Margaret and Jonathan Yeates, ...	1776	M.L. .	90
, Mary and Joseph Henderson, ...	1764	M.L. .	21
„ Matthew, Blackpitts, co. Dub., weaver, . .	1733	I. .	271
„ Matthew, Mitchers Mount, Santry, co. Dub., . .	1778	W. .	179
„ Michael, Dublin, ...	1726	O.W. .	—
„ Michael, Leixlip, co. Kild., dealer, . . .	1792	I. .	257
„ Michael and Mary Elinor Anderson, . . .	1778	M.L. .	216
„ Michael and Judith Hapson, ...	1792	M.L. .	279
„ Peter and Prudence Nesbitt, ...	1767	M.L. .	352
„ Regina and Thomas Popham, ...	1782	M.L. .	56
„ Richard, Carrickmines, co. Dub., yeoman, . .	1707	I. .	**142
„ Richard, Kilmashoge, co. Dub., farmer, . .	1778	I. .	191
„ Rickard and Mary Giles, ...	1754	M.L. .	315
„ Thomas, Dublin, dairyman, ...	1685	Cav. .	**104
„ Thomas, Rathfarnham, co. Dub., yeoman, .	1685	I. .	**104
„ Thomas, chief baron, Exchequer, . . .	1730 .	O.W. .	—
„ Thomas, a minor, ...	1756	L.T. .	431
„ Thomas and Sarah Lindsay, ...	1795	M.L. .	144
„ Walter, Island-bridge, ...	1752	I. .	191
„ William, Thomas-st., mariner, . . .	1748	W. .	464
„ William and Mary Bond, ...	1751	M.L. .	146
„ William and Martha M'Mourtrie, . . .	1761	M.L. .	259
Daly, Andrew, Dublin, musician, ...	1782	W. .	9
„ Ann and John Supple, ...	1768	M.L. .	409
„ Anne and Epaphroditus Andrews, . . .	1790	M.L. .	112
„ Arthur and Henrietta Bradish, . . .	1784	M.L. .	175
„ Charles and Jane True (*alias* Hill), . . .	1753	M.L. .	237
„ Charlotte and Joshua Dixon, . . .	1790	M.L. .	59
„ Christopher, Pill-lane, grocer, . . .	1796	W. .	219
„ Connor (Daley), Ballyowen, co. Dub., . .	1645	L.S. .	53 D
„ Cuthbert and Ismena French, . . .	1797	M.L. .	248
„ Denis Bowes and Mary Charlotte Ponsonby, .	1780	M.L. .	320
„ Dorinda (*alias* French) and James Mahon, .	1794	M.L. '	392
„ Dorothea (*alias* French) and John French. .	1775	M.L. .	215
„ Elinor and Randall Myers, ...	1784	M.L. .	177
„ Elizabeth and Charles Forster, . . .	1720	M.L.B. .	—
„ Elizabeth and John Mills, ...	1792	M.L. .	234
„ Francis, Dolphins-barn, clothier, . . .	1750	I. .	80
„ Harriot and Thomas Coates, ...	1795	M.L. .	73
„ Hugh, Bride-st., ...	1780	O.W. .	—
„ John, Thomas-st., maltster, ...	1676	Ren. .	**125

Extract from the Act or Grant Books, and index to original Wills, of the diocese of Dublin to the year 1800. Appendix to the 26th Rept. DKPRI Dublin 1895.

8.2 Administrations

If a person died without making a will, the Prerogative and Consistorial courts had responsibility for deciding on the distribution of the deceased's property to family and creditors. Having made its decision the court acted by appointing an administrator (usually a next of kin or major creditor) to look after and distribute the estate of the deceased in the manner set down. The administrator entered a bond for a sum of money as surety that he would do so (hence Administration Bonds). Most of the records of these courts perished in the 1922 fire. The following survive:

(a) *Surviving Administrations:* Those available are the Prerogative Administrations of 1684-88, 1748-51 and 1839.

(b) *Abstracts of Administrations:* In many of the collections listed in 8.1(b) both wills and administrations have been abstracted. Abstracts of approximately 5000 pre-1802 administrations were made by Betham. The originals are at the PRO while an indexed copy is in the Genealogical Office. These abstracts contain deceased's name, address and occupation, date of grant and to whom made. The Prerogative Court of Canterbury also granted administrations and these are included with the wills in the records for 1828-39 available at the PRO (q.v)

(c) *Administration Bonds:* (see above) No original Dublin bonds survived the Public Record Office fire.

8.3 Marriage Licences

Civil registration of Irish marriages began in 1845 for Church of Ireland marriages, and in 1864 for other denominations. Until their dis-establishment in 1857, the Church of Ireland were responsible for granting permission to marry. The church used two methods to ensure that neither party had already been married. (1) publishing of "Banns" i.e. giving 3 weeks public notice of intention to marry so that objections could be made or (2) marriage license bonds i.e. the groom (usually) would lodge a sum of money as surety that there was no reason not to marry. This sum was theoretically to insure the church against any damages which might be sought at a later date if there was an existing impediment to the marriage. Because publishing of banns was cheapest, it was also the most common form of marriage.

There are few records of banns. Likewise the original marriage license bonds have not survived. However, indexes and some abstracts of marriage license bonds and grants (i.e. the official permission to marry) survive. The indexes give the names of bride and groom and the year of the marriage.

The following are available:

Indexes: Dublin (1672) PRO; SLC 100,867

Original Bonds: Dublin (1749-1813) indexed by males surnames beginning with A only. PRO; SLC 101,770

Abstracts: Fisher's Abstracts (1638-1800), indexed separately for bride and groom by surname gives groom's name, address, bride's name and address and date of marriage: GO MS 134-138.

Listing of Licences: Dublin (1638-1800). Phillip's listing, by both bride and groom's surnames, of all marriage licences granted and intended place of marriage. GO MS 473-475. SLC 100,227.

8.4 Major Repositories of Will and Administration Records

Public Record Office: This is the largest collection of Irish wills anywhere. It includes wills which survived the 1922 fire, copies and originals which have been deposited since, and various collections of will abstracts. The following are the surviving will books held in the PRO:

Prerogative Wills for the years 1664-84; 1706-08 (A-W); 1726-8 (A-W); 1728-9 (A-W); 1777 (A-L); 1813 (K-Z); 1834 (A-E).

Consistorial Wills: the individual consistorial courts varied as to the care which they took of wills deposited with them. In 1857 the PRO was entrusted with keeping the will documents. When they began to assemble the wills, the number of wills actually received from each court varied greatly. None produced all the wills they should have had, few provided many wills before 1780, and some produced very few from any period. Only one consistorial will survived the 1922 fire and none of the Dublin will-books. All of the indexes survive (see p. 72) and are available at the PRO.

Of particular note among the PRO's collection of abstracts is the Betham Prerogative Will Abstracts. In 1860 Sir William Betham organized the indexing of Prerogative wills according to testator's names. He also wrote out brief genealogical abstracts of almost all the pre 1800 wills, amounting to some 37,500 abstracts. These are held in the PRO. The general card index in the PRO covers the wills and will copies and most abstract collections: e.g. the Greene (e.g. wills of Greene family members) and Thrift collections.

The Irish Will Registers compiled by the Inland Revenue Commissioners, London are available from 1828-39 (except part of 1834). They give the names and addresses of testator and executors, dates of will, decease and probate and the main legacies and names of beneficiaries. This is a very valuable reference for the period 1828-39. The Indexes to Irish Will Registers compiled by the Inland Revenue Commissioners in London for the years 1828-79 are also available in the PRO. These give the name and address of testator and executor (often a family member).

Genealogical Office: the GO collection is mainly pre-1800 and many are arranged in series dealing with particular families. These are referenced in Hayes' index (see below). The GO collection is not indexed and thus it is somewhat difficult to determine its exact contents. A general index of their holdings is in Analecta Hibernica Vol. 17.

Registry of Deeds: The Registry of Deeds has a collection of almost 1500 wills deposited with them in connection with land transfer particularly regarding disputed legacies of land. These wills have been abstracted and published by the Irish Manuscripts Commission as **Registry of Deeds, Dublin, Abstracts of Wills**. Vol 1. 1708-1745 and Vol 2. 1746-1788. Ed P.B. Eustace (1954-56); and Vol 3. 1785-1832, Eds. E. Ellis and P.B. Eustace (1984).

National Library of Ireland: There are many collections of wills relating to specific families and areas held here. They are not separately indexed. However Hayes' **Manuscript Sources for the History of Irish Civilizationn** idexes all NLI holdings by name, area etc.

CHAPTER 9

Gravestone Inscriptions

These can be a very useful source of information as, in many cases, they indicate relationships or give the ages, or birthdates of those interred. They are extensively researched in some counties e.g. Wicklow, Wexford and virtually unresearched in others. Twenty-two Dublin graveyards have been indexed. The records list the name of the graveyard and the place of publication or availability of the transcriptions. Unfortunately the name of the graveyard is not always the name of the town or even of a local townland. Graveyards are often on ancient monastic sites which predate other boundary names. The location of most, however, is determinable with the "Index to Townlands etc." (see p. 12).

Chapelizod: Ir. Gen. 5(4), 1977, p. 490-505.

Cloghran: History and Description of Santry and Cloghran Parishes, by Rev. Benjamin W. Adams, 1883.

Dalkey: Ir. Gen. 5(2) 1975, p. 250-255.

Dublin City: Christ Church Cathedral: Inscriptions on the Monuments in Christ Church Cathedral, Dublin, by Rev. John Finlayson, 1878.

St. Andrew's, Westland Row (names on coffin plates): Ir. Gen. 5(1), 1974, p. 131-139.

SS. Michael & John (names on coffin plates): Ir. Gen. 5(3), 1976, p. 368-369.

St. Paul (C of I): RSAI, 104 (1974).

Esker: Ir. Gen. 6(1), p. 54-58.

This Stone is placed here by Sir Compton Domvile Bar[t] in memory of an old and faithful servant, Elizabeth Canavan, who departed this life 21st January 1815, aged eighty years.

Here lyeth the Body of Richard Murphy, who departed this life on the 29th of October 1712, being the 64th year of his age. Here also lyeth the body of Bridget Wise, Wife of the s[d] Richard Murphy, who departed this life y[e] 20th of April 1691, and 3 of their children lyeth heer.

Here lyeth the body of Joshua Smith, who departed this life the 14 of June 1707, as also nine of his children, with several other of his relations.

This Stone and Burial place belongs to Catherine Marvin for her and her posterity. She died June 1788. Aged 50 Years.

There lieth the body of John Mountaine, Who Died October the 6th 1749. Aged 67 Years. Also two of his Children.

This Stone was erected here by Thomas Foskey in Memory of his Father John Foskey and his Mother Mary Foskey of Ballymun and Parish of Santry and County of Dublin, Far[r]. Here Lieth the Body of Rich[d] Foskey Son of John Foskey, who dept[d] this Life 23rd July Anno Domini 1768, Aged 70 Years.

Sacred to the memory of Jane Anderson, Wife of John Anderson, who departed this life 19th Dec[r] 1846. Aged 63 Years.

This Stone was Erected by M[r] John Clinton of Bell Curris in Memory of his Wife Eleanor Clinton, who Dep[d] this life Sep[r] 2[d] 1772, aged 31 Years. Here Also Lieth the Body of John Clinton, Son to the above John Clinton, who departed this life Dec[r] the 1st 1773, aged 15 Years.

This Stone and Burial Place is the Property of Thomas Quinn and his posterity of Newtown in the Parish of Coolough. Here layeth the Body of James Quinn, who died 8th of March 1728, Aged 65 Years. Also the Body of James, son of the above Thomas Quinn, who died 3rd of July 1763. Aged 27 Years.

Example of gravestone inscriptions from Santry churchyard. In "History & Description of Santry & Cloghran Parishes" by Rev. B.W. Adams, 1883.

Kilbride: Ir. Gen. 6(3) 1982, p. 378-381.

Kilmactalway: Ir. Gen. 6(3) 1982, p. 378-381.

Kilmahuddrick: Ir. Gen. 6(3) 1982, p. 378-381.

Killiney (old Graveyard):   Ir. Gen. 4(6) 1973, p. 647-648

Kill o' the Grange: Ir. Gen. 4(5), 1972, p. 507-514.

Leixlip: Ir. Gen. 4(2), 1969, p. 110-116.

Loughtown Lr: Ir. Gen. 6(3) 1982, p. 378-381.

Lucan: Ir. Gen. 5(6) 1976, p. 763-767.

Monkstown: Ir. Gen. 4(3) 1970, p. 201-202, and 4(4) 1971.

Newcastle: Ir. Gen. 6(2) 1981, p. 219-226.

Palmerstown: Ir. Gen. 4(5) 1978, p. 650-653.

Rathcoole: Ir. Gen. 6(4) 1983, p. 523-525.

Santry: "History and Description of Santry and Cloghran Parishes", by Rev. Benjamin W. Adams, 1883.

Tallaght: Ir. Gen. 4(1) 1968, p 29-36.

Taney: "The Parish of Taney", by F. Elrington Ball, 1895.

CHAPTER 10

Archives, Research Services and Local History Sources

10.1 Archives:

The main archives in which the records relevant to Dublin families are kept are as follows:

National library of Ireland (NLI) Kildare St. Dublin 2. Ph: 765521. Holdings include: Griffiths Valuation Survey i.e. list of householders in each county (see p. 21); Microfilm copies of most Catholic Registers; Local and Commercial Directories (see p. 52); Microfilm and original copies of Irish Newspapers (see p. 31); estate papers and records, maps, old photographs and many other sources.

Public Record Office of Ireland (PRO), Four Courts, Dublin 7. Ph (01)733833. Holds the original Tithe Applotment books (see p. 31); Census returns for 1901, 1911 and the surviving parts of other censuses (see p. 19); copies and originals of some of surviving Church of Ireland Parish Registers (see also Representative Church Body library). Also many manuscripts of relevance to family and local history such as Estate records, Court records and other Government papers.

The Registry of Deeds, Henrietta Street, Dublin 1. Records of property transactions since 1708.

State Paper Office, Dublin Castle, Dublin 2. Records of the British administration of Ireland. Relevant records include lists of convicts who were transported, records of 1798 Rebellion, Fenian Rising and many others.

Representative Church Body Library (RCB), Braemor Park, Rathgar, Dublin 14. ph(01) 979979. Holds some surviving Church of Ireland Parish records, records of the Church of Ireland clergy and other records and books relevant to the Church of Ireland.

Genealogical Office (GO), 42 Kildare, St. Dublin 2 ph (01)608670. This office incorporates the State Heraldic Museum, and the Office of the Chief Herald. The institution has been in existence continuously since 1552, assigning and ratifying coats of arms for individuals and institutions. The office has a large range of material on family pedigrees, wills, funeral entries (ie biographies of noblemen who died from 1552 to 1700) and operates a genealogical research service.

Registrar-General's Office, 8-11 Lombard St., Dublin 2. ph(01) 711000. This office contains all of the official records of births marriages and deaths for all counties since records began in 1864. It also has Church of Ireland (Protestant or Episcopalian) marriage records from April 1845 to 1864. A public research room is available where the indexes to these records can be consulted.

Religious Society of Friends Historical Library (i.e. Quakers), Swanbrook House, Morehampton Road, Dublin 4, has records of Quaker meeting houses in Munster, Leinster and Connaught. Research is conducted for a fee.

Trinity College Library (TCD), Dublin 2. Ph (01) 772941. This library has a fine collection of Manuscripts, Newspapers and other sources.

Royal Irish Academy (RIA), 19 Dawson St., Dublin. Ph (01) 762570 has a large collection of manuscript and printed sources.

Gilbert Library, Pearse Street, Dublin 2. Tel: (01) 777662. This is the best collection of books on Dublin and has copies of many other records relevant to Dublin. It is part of the Dublin Public Library of which there are 37 branches in the county.

10.2 Research Services

The following will perform research on Irish family records for a fee:

Genealogical Office, Kildare Street, Dublin 2. Ph (01) 608670.

Genealogical and Historical Research, Farnham House, 4 Henrietta Street, Dublin 1. P.O. Box No. 1501.

Hibernian Research Co. Ltd., Windsor House, 22 Windsor Road, Rathmines, Dublin 6. Tel (01) 966522.

Irish Research Services, 60 Pinewood Avenue, Dublin 11.

Dr J. Ryan, 4 Spencer Villas, Glenageary, Co Dublin. Ph (01) 806228.

Dr Christine Kinealy, 10 Grosvenor Road, Rathmines, Dublin 6.

10.3 Local History Societies and Journals

There is great interest in the local history of Dublin as is shown by the numbers of local history societies listed. Researchers may be interested to correspond with such societies in order to place queries in their newsletters or journals, or indeed to offer information.

BALBRIGGAN HISTORICAL AND CULTURAL SOCIETY
Mr Michael Kennedy, 45 Clonard Court, Balbriggan, Co. Dublin.

BALDOYLE HISTORICAL SOCIETY
Mr Barney Walsh, Stapolin Lawns, Baldoyle, Co. Dublin.

DONABATE HISTORICAL SOCIETY
Mr Rob Browne, 5 New St., Skerries, Co. Dublin.

DUBLIN FAMILY HISTORY SOCIETY
Synod Hall, Christchurch, St Michael's Hill, Dublin 2.

DUBLIN ARCHAEOLOGICAL SOCIETY
Ms Jane Behan, 54 Meadowbrook, Baldoyle, Dublin 13

CLONDALKIN HISTORY SOCIETY
Mr Padraig Murphy, 13 New Rd., , Clondalkin, Co Dublin.

DOLPHIN'S BARN HISTORICAL SOCIETY
Ms Catherine Scuffil, c/o Public Library, Dolphin's Barn, Dublin 8.

DUN LAOGHAIRE BOROUGH HISTORICAL SOCIETY
Mr Dermot Dwyer, 35 Gleneageary Woods, Dun Laoghaire, Co Dublin

FOXROCK LOCAL HISTORY CLUB
Mr Liam Clare, 73 Clonkeen Drive, Foxrock, Dublin 18

LUCAN HISTORICAL SOCIETY
Mr Glascott Symes, c/o The King's Hospital, Palmerston, Dublin 20.

LUSK HISTORICAL SOCIETY
Mr Tom Seever, Moylough, The Commons, Lusk, Co. Dublin.

MOUNT MERRION HISTORICAL SOCIETY
Mrs Evanna Kennedy, 16 Wilson Road, Mount Merrion, Blackrock, Co. Dublin.

OLD DUBLIN SOCIETY
City Assembly House, 58 South William Street, Dublin 2. (Publishers of **Dublin Historical Record**)

OLD FINGAL SOCIETY
Brendan & Doreen Scally, Shanowen Drive, Santry, Co. Dublin.

OLD MALAHIDE SOCIETY
Mr Tom O'Shea, 4 Woodlawn, Dublin Road, Malahide, Co. Dublin.

OLD SKERRIES SOCIETY
Mr Eugene Coyle, 11 Holmpatrick Terrace, Skerries, Co. Dublin.

RATHMICHAEL HISTORICAL SOCIETY
Mr R. Goodbody, 35 Corke Abbey, Bray, Co. Wicklow.

SWORDS HISTORICAL SOCIETY
Mrs Bernadette Marks, Mount Gorry, Swords, Co. Dublin.

TALLAGHT HISTORICAL SOCIETY
Ms J. Lavin, 25 Parkwood Lawn, Aylesbury, Tallaght, Co. Dublin.

10.4 Relevant Journals

The local journals in Dublin include **Dublin Historical Record**, published by the Old Dublin Society and **Reportorium Novum**, which reports mainly Dublin Diocesan history. Apart from the local journals there are also many journals which cover local, or family, history in all of Ireland. These include: **Analecta Hibernica, Irish Ancestor, Irish Genealogist, Gaelic Gleanings**, and the **Journal of the Royal Society of Antiquarians of Ireland.** The articles in these journals include detailed histories of specific parishes or townlands, information on local families and institutions, and accounts of the local effects of various events. Many will accept queries from researchers. In short, therefore, all sorts of local historical detail is available which may either explain certain events in an ancestor's history, or point towards other avenues for research.

CHAPTER 11

Miscellaneous Sources

This section lists other sources which provide background information relevant to Dublin family history research. They vary from general histories of Dublin to more specialized accounts of specific areas or records.

The Huguenots in Dublin, Dublin Hist. Rec., 8, 1945-6, 110-34.

The Manor of Lucan and the Restoration Land Settlement, 1660-1688. Dublin Hist. Rec., 21, 1966-67, 139-143.

Succession lists of parish priests in Dublin Diocese 1771-1960. Dublin Hist. Rec., 3(1), 1962, p. 178-190.

Adams, B.W., **History and Description of the Parishes of Santry and Cloghran.** Dublin 1883.

Ball, F.E., **The Vicinity of the International Exhibition in Dublin. An Historical sketch of the Pembroke Township.** 53p. Blackrock, Co Dublin, Carraig Books, 1983 (Facsimile Reprint).

Ball, F.E. & Hamilton, E., **The Parish of Taney: A History of Dundrum, near Dublin and its neighbourhood.** Dublin, Hodges Figgis & Co. Ltd. (1895).

Ball, F.E., **A History of the county Dublin: its people, parishes and antiquities from the earliest times to the close of the 18th century:**
Part 1 Dublin Thom. 1902
Part 2 Dublin Thom. 1903
Part 3 Dublin Thom. 1905
Part 4 Dublin Thom. 1906
Part 5 University Press (1917) (RSAI)
Part 6 University Press (1920) (RSAI)
(All reprinted: Dublin, Gill & McMillan 1979).

Cosgrave, D., **North Dublin City and County,** (Dublin, 1909). Reprinted: Dublin 1977.

Craig, M., **Dublin 1660-1860,** 362pp. Cresset Press, 1952.

THE PARISH OF TANEY:

A HISTORY OF DUNDRUM,

NEAR DUBLIN,

AND ITS NEIGHBOURHOOD.

BY

FRANCIS ELRINGTON BALL

AND

EVERARD HAMILTON, B.A., Univ. of Dub.,

Member Royal Society of Antiquaries of Ireland

DUBLIN:

HODGES, FIGGIS, & CO., Ltd., GRAFTON ST.,

PUBLISHERS TO THE UNIVERSITY.

1895.

D'Alton, J. **The History of Co. Dublin** (Dublin 1838), (reprinted Cork 1976).

Dixon, F.E., **The Dublin Tailors and their Hall**. Dublin Hist. Rec. 22 (1968).

Fitzpatrick, S.A., **Dublin: A Historical & Topographical Account of the City**. (Dublin 1907), Reprinted Cork, 1977.

Gilbert, J.J.: **A History of the City of Dublin**, 3 Vols. (reprinted Dublin 1972).

Gillespie, E., **The Liberties of Dublin**. Dublin 1973.

Handcock, W.D., **The History of Tallaght** (Printed Dublin 1876) Reprinted Cork 1976.

Harrison, W., **Memorable Dublin Houses**. (First Published Dublin 1890). Reprinted Dublin, S.R. Publishers, 1971.

Joyce, W. St John, **The Neighbourhood of Dublin**. Dublin 1921.

Kennedy, T. (ed.), **Victorian Dublin**. Dublin, 1980.

MacGiolla Phadraig, B., **History of Terenure**, 76pp. Dublin, Veritas (1955).

Maxwell, Constantia. **Dublin under the Georges** (First Published, London 1936). Reprinted Dublin 1979.

McCready, Rev. C.T., **Dublin Street Names**. (1892) Reprinted Blackrock (Co Dublin), Carraig Books, 1975.

O'Broin, S., **The Book of Finglas**. Dublin, 1980.

O'Driscoll, J., **A History of Castleknock & District**, Dublin 1977.

Redmond, B., **The Story of Dublin City and County**. Dublin, Browne & Nolan (1927).

Warburton, J.W., Whitelaw, Rev. J., and Walsh, Rev. R.: **A History of the City of Dublin**, London 1818.

Webb, J.J., **The Guilds of Dublin**. Dublin, Three Candles (1929).

White, F., **Report & Observations on the poor of Dublin**. Dublin, 1833.

DUBLIN.   **3**

it in so many different ways, and with such a variety of objects—that I run but little risk of incurring censure by passing it over with a very hasty and superficial notice. Dublin is indeed a fine city; but it is a city of lamentable contrasts. If the stranger be forcibly struck by the number and magnificence of the public buildings, and the general beauty of some of the streets, he is sure to be no less forcibly moved by the very different character of those parts which are termed "the Liberties." Here, narrow streets, houses without windows or doors, and several families crowded together beneath the same roof, present a picture of ruin, disease, poverty, filth, and wretchedness, of which they who have not witnessed it are unable to form a competent idea. Dublin, I have said, is a city of lamentable contrasts: so is London; but the contrasts of Dublin are brought more immediately together than those of the English metropolis. When Dublin presents a scene of the most enlivening gaiety, numbers of miserable beings may be seen lying half naked, and apparently half dead from cold

A description of Dublin in 1835 from "The Miseries and Beauties of Ireland" by Jonathan Binns (1837).

32   *Dublin Street Names*

Dopping-ct. (Golden-la.) 1776.
From the family of Anthony *Dopping* (1643-81), Bishop of
Meath.

Dorset-str. (Bolton-str.) 1756.
From Lionel Cranfield Sackville (cf. Sackville-str.), 1st
Duke of *Dorset* (1688-1765), L.L. 1731-37, 1751-55.
Previously called Drumcondra-la., 1728.

Dowker's-la. (New-str.) 1766, = Ducker's-la.
Is not this the same as Tucker's-la. (New-str.) 1756?

Draper's-ct. (S. Nicholas-str.) 1756.
Perhaps from one Edward *Draper*, mentioned in the Register of S. Nicholas Within, in the year 1681.

Draw-br.   See Bridges (Grand Canal).

Drogheda-str. 1728.
From Henry Moore, cr. in 1661, 1st Earl of *Drogheda*,--
whence also Henry-str., Moore-str., Earl-str. N., Off-la.
(Cf. Meath-str., etc.)
[Similarly in London, George-str., Villiers-str., Duke-str.,
and Buckingham-str.,were so named from George Villiers,
Duke of Buckingham. (Jesse's London, ii. 237.)]
It is now called Sackville-str. up. and lr.

Drumcondra-la. 1697.
From its leading to Drumcondra.
It is now called Dorset-str., q.v.

Drury-la. (Barrack-str.) 1766. [Harris.]

Drury-la. (Exchequer-str.) 1766.
Called Butter-la., little, q.v., in 1728. The lane having been
widened by the South City Market Company, was called
Drury-*street* in 1887.
Rev. John *Drury*, sch. T.C.D., 1735, was curate of Donny-
brook, 1753.

*Extract from "Dublin Street names—Dated and Explained" by Rev.
C.T. McCready (1892), reprinted 1975, Carraig Books, Dublin.*

List of Abbreviations

Add.	Additional
Anal. Hib.	Analecta Hibernica
b.	birth/born
BL	British Library
c.	circa
C of I	Church of Ireland (Protestant or Episcopalian)
Co.	County
d.	death/died (indicates burial in Church records)
DKPRI	Deputy Keeper of Public Records of Ireland (Report of ...)
DU	Dublin (Diocese)
Dublin Hist. Rec.	Dublin Historical Record
Ed.	Edited
Gen.	Genealogy/ical
GO	Genealogical Office
Hist.	Historical
Ir. Anc.	Irish Ancestor
Ir. Gen.	Irish Genealogist
J.	Journal
J. Ass. Pres. Mem. Dead.	Journal of the Association for the Preservation of Memorials of the Dead.
J. Kildare Arch.	Journal of the Kildare Archaeological & Historical Society
m.	Marriage/married
Misc.	Miscellaneous

MP	Member of Parliament (i.e. Westminster)
Ms/s	Manuscript/s
n.d.	not dated/no date
NLI	National Library of Ireland
No/s.	Number/s
N.S.	New Series
p/p	Page/s
Parish Reg. Soc.	Parish Register Society
Parl.	Parliament/ary
Ph.	Phone
PHSA	Presbyterian Historical Society Archives
PRO	Public Record Office
PRO (M)	Public Record Office (microfilm)
PRONI	Public Record Office of Northern Ireland
Pub.	Published/er
QUB	Queens University, Belfast
RC	Roman Catholic
RCB	Representative Church Body
Ref	Reference
RIA	Royal Irish Academy
RSAI	Royal Society of Antiquarians of Ireland (Journal of)
SLC	Genealogical Library, Salt Lake City
SPO	State Paper Office
TCD	Trinity College Dublin
Vol/s.	Volume/s

List of Illustrations

General Index